THE SUN·MAID® COOKBOOK

BROUGHT TO YOU BY
SUN·MAID GROWERS
OF
CALIFORNIA

A Benjamin Company Book

Recipe Development: Judy Hobbs
Martha S. Reynolds

Color Photography: Walter Storck

Typography: A-Line, Milwaukee

Prepared and produced by The Benjamin Company, Inc.
One Westchester Plaza
Elmsford, New York 10523

ISBN: 0-87502-070-4
Library of Congress Card Catalog Number: 79-54948

Printed in the United States of America
Second Printing: July, 1981

Sun•Maid® is a registered trademark of
Sun•Maid Growers of California, Kingsburg, California 93631.

Table of Contents

The Romance of Raisins

Since 1490 B.C.

The raisin played an important role in the history of civilization. The Bible, for instance, tells that after Abigail had bestowed upon King David gifts which included 100 clusters of raisins, she became his wife. We know of raisins being sun-dried from grapes as long ago as 1490 B.C., and they were important in the nomadic commerce of the ancient Middle East. Early Greeks and Romans decorated places of worship with raisins, and they were given as prizes to winners of sporting contests. As absurd as it seems, Roman physicians even prescribed raisin potions to cure almost all ailments — from mushroom poisoning to old age. Emperor Augustus feasted on small birds stuffed with raisins (that would still be a tasty gourmet dish on our tables). The mighty general Hannibal fed them to his troops as they crossed the Alps, and today mountain climbers, hikers, athletes, and non-athletes of all ages enjoy the delicious taste of raisins and the quick nutritious boost of energy they provide.

One of nature's great convenience foods, raisins are an easily movable feast perfect for today's life styles: they need no peeling, no preserving, and there's nothing left to throw away. They are light and easily carried and can be eaten alone or with many other foods.

Raisins have long been a cherished American favorite. Over a dozen recipes calling for raisins appeared in *American Cookery* by Amelia Simmons, the first cookbook written in America, published in 1796. For such recipes as "A Minced Pie of Beef," "A Nice Indian Pudding," "A Bread Pudding," and "A Rich Cake," Amelia Simmons advised that "All raisins should be stoned (pitted)" — a time-consuming task that Sun-Maid eliminates for us by cultivating mostly seedless grapes. (The seeds in the Muscat variety of grape are removed by mechanical processing.)

Somehow raisins did not make the westward trek with our pioneering ancestors, although all along the California coast Spanish missionaries were growing grapes for wine making. Fortunately raisins were rediscovered by chance in the fertile San Joaquin Valley, where some forty-niners had settled to farm after the Gold Rush. In 1851 a rancher planted Egyptian Muscat vines, which bear a grape suitable for raisin-making, and in the next few years additional suitable European varieties were planted, but the grapes were consumed only fresh or as wine.

Established in California in 1873

Our modern raisin industry was born in 1873 when a devastating September heat spell shriveled the grapes on the vines. One enterprising grower unfamiliar with the resulting ancient staple shipped his "dried grapes" to San Francisco anyway, where an equally unknowing and enterprising storekeeper called them "Peruvian delicacies" and quickly sold out his supply!

These early settlers wisely adapted to grape growing the techniques they'd used for channeling water to their mining sites. They carved canals to bring water from the nearby High Sierras down to the valley floor, where only about 10 inches of rain fall each year. An extensive irrigation network has since grown up around these canals. The hard work and skill of growers, pickers, and processors, along with the long, hot, dry summers, mild winters, plus an abundant water supply from the nearby mountains, enable this rich valley to yield the entire U.S. raisin crop. This fertile area, with its unique combination of soil and climatic conditions within 25 miles of Sun-Maid's plant, also provide about one-third of the world's supply of raisins.

From a few vines brought to California by William Thompson, an Englishman, comes 95 percent of our California raisins and our favorite table grapes as well. The sweet-flavored thin-skinned Thompson Seedless is ideal for making into raisins. ("That grape which was born to be a raisin," one writer called it.) While Sun-Maid packs and distributes four types of raisins to supermarkets and grocery stores throughout the country, the majority of the raisins sold to consumers are natural sun-dried Thompson Seedless, which are packaged in the familiar red carton or bag, for use as either an ingredient or as a snack food. Another raisin that Sun-Maid markets is the Golden Seedless Thompson. The attractive light color and distinct taste of these raisins make them suitable for snacking as well as for baking fruit cakes and other special dishes. Sun-Maid Muscat raisins are large, dark, and extra sweet raisins which derive from Muscat grapes. Their exceptional fruitiness makes them particularly satisfying in a variety of recipes. Zante Currants are tiny raisins with a unique sweet taste that makes them the perfect addition or accent to entrées, salads, desserts, and baked goods.

Today the cooperative association of over 2,000 growers known as Sun-Maid owns the world's largest and most modern raisin processing facility in Kingsburg, California. Most of these growers are small, family farmers. The average farm size for the Sun-Maid grower is about 37 acres.

Lorraine Collett Petersen, The Sun-Maid herself, at a celebration of the 60th anniversary of the Sun-Maid Growers of California.

The Sun-Maid

The Sun-Maid girl herself, whose smile has beamed from the familiar red packages for over 65 years, is Lorraine Collett Petersen, who was spotted wearing her red sunbonnet in Fresno's 1915 Raisin Day Parade. She was a schoolgirl also working as a raisin seeder and packer. Mrs. Petersen still lives in Fresno and, although her name is not widely known, her face has probably graced every American home as well as homes in 50 foreign countries many times.

Quality Grapes Make Quality Raisins

Grape cultivation begins with planting vines that will bear fruit three or four years later. When they start yielding grapes, the vines require expert pruning every year. They also need water that will soak their roots deeply in spring and throughout a long, hot, dry summer. Warm spring days draw out the first buds. Soon there appear tiny clusters of grapes that need the hot summer to grow and sweeten. All the grapes in a region ripen at once, in late August or early September, and must be picked carefully and quickly by hand. Then, for Sun-Maid® Raisins, the clusters of grapes are spread out to dry in the sun. Growers devoutly hope for continued dry weather during this three-to-four-week drying season, because rain at this time could significantly reduce the harvest.

After the hot California sun reduces the moisture content to about 12 percent, grapes turn into raisins. Then come frequent washings, careful inspections by Sun-Maid quality control people, several U.S. Department of Agriculture inspections, and packaging before Sun-MaidRaisins start on their way to you. At every stage of this processing, of course, the raisins must pass Sun-Maid's exacting standards of quality. It takes about four and a half pounds of grapes to yield one pound of Sun-Maid® Raisins which, fortunately, retains all the original nutritive values of the grapes.

The raisin is a wonderful nugget of pure food energy, containing 70 percent natural fruit sugar in a form the body easily digests. Raisins also provide many other essential nutrients: iron, in highly usable form, especially important for women, children, and all vegetarians; worthwhile amounts of potassium (needed by all of us and particularly by people taking diuretics); and of phosphorus, calcium, magnesium, and fiber. They are low in sodium, have only traces of fat, and contain no cholesterol. Raisins can be useful to dieters and to parents who prefer not to give candy to their children, for a small number of raisins can satisfy the craving for something sweet and a quarter cup contains only 125 calories.

The combination of natural fruit sugar and low moisture in Sun-Maid® Raisins means no preservatives are needed.

Proper storage of raisins is important. High temperatures will cause raisins to dry out and humid conditions can cause the sugar in the fruit to crystallize. However, under cool, controlled conditions of storage, raisins will retain their flavor, color and nutritive value for up to two years. Once a package has been opened, the raisins should be stored in an air-tight container and refrigerated. If convenient, raisins can be stored in the freezer for even longer periods of time. They thaw quickly at room temperature. In the event that the raisins form sugar crystals or become dry due to improper storage, they can be softened by soaking in hot water for about 15 minutes. Soaking will dissolve the crystals and restore moisture to the fruit.

The Versatile Fruit

Many cooks distribute the fruit and its flavor throughout prepared food by first chopping the raisins. For easy chopping, toss the raisins in vegetable oil, using 1 teaspoon of oil per cup of raisins. Then chop by using a long-bladed knife, blender, or food processor.

Raisins can be used in a number of different ways. For example, they can be baked in cakes or cookies, stirred into yogurts or puddings, sprinkled on cereals or ice cream, kneaded into bread dough, or plumped in fruit juice or other beverages to serve over cake, ice cream, or gingerbread.

In addition to the breads, cookies, puddings, cakes, and sauces you've already prepared and liked, you might enjoy trying various South American dishes that include raisins with ground meat. In Greek cooking, too, raisins are used in lamb and rice dishes, and in (Asian) Indian meals they are standard accompaniments to curried food. And of course it's part of the romance of raisins to remember that they're a vital ingredient in many traditional wedding cakes — such as the only one presented in Mrs. Beeton's *English Cookery,* first published in 1861 and long a classic cookbook in the whole English-speaking world. Perhaps it was the 3 pounds of raisins in this cake that made Mrs. Beeton add after the simple title "Wedding Cake," "(Very Good)"!

We think you'll be saying "Very Good," too, when you make tasty and nutritious Sun-Maid® Raisins part of your daily nourishment.

Sun-Maid® Seedless Raisins

Sun-Maid Seedless raisins, found in familiar red packages, are made from fully ripened and naturally sweet Thompson Seedless grapes. These raisins are dried naturally by the sun and are the most popular raisins sold in food stores today.

Sun-Maid® Golden Seedless Raisins

Sun-Maid Golden Seedless raisins, packaged in golden cartons, are also made from Thompson Seedless grapes. After being picked from the vines, these grapes are oven-dried and then are sulphured to help retain their distinctively attractive golden color, so suitable for those special recipes.

Sun-Maid® Puffed Seeded Muscat Raisins

Sun-Maid Muscat raisins, packaged in blue foil cartons, are sun-dried from the large, dark, extra sweet Muscat of Alexandria grapes. The seeds are removed by an ingenious mechanical process. Muscats possess an exceptional fruity flavor and are excellent for quality baking. Only a few Muscat raisins are produced, so the supply is limited.

Sun-Maid® Zante Currants

Sun-Maid Zante Currants, packaged in bright orange cartons, are miniature sun-dried seedless raisins made from Black Corinth grapes. These tiny raisins are dark in color and tangy in flavor. They should not be confused with the berry of the same name common to the eastern United States. "Currant" is a mutation of the grape name "Corinth," and "Zante" is the English name of the Greek island of Zakinthos, where the grapes first grew.

Appealing Appetizers
Good Beginnings for Great Meals

What better way to tempt the appetite than with these dishes made with raisins and other dried fruit? Nutritious and almost irresistible, any opener made with Sun-Maid fruit will tease the palate and please the inner person!

Spicy Dip for Vegetables   1 1/4 cups

Every gathering needs a perky vegetable dip. Our low-calorie offering will perk up crisp vegetables and your guests' appetites.

1/4 cup Sun-Maid® Seedless
    Raisins
1 cup cream-style cottage
    cheese
2 tablespoons cider vinegar
1/2 small onion, cut up
1 teaspoon chili powder

1/2 to 3/4 teaspoon
    curry powder
3/4 teaspoon salt
1/8 teaspoon freshly
    ground black pepper
Crisp fresh vegetables
    for dipping

Place raisins in a small bowl and cover with hot tap water. Let stand 10 minutes.

Meanwhile, in blender container, combine cottage cheese, vinegar, onion, chili powder, curry, salt, and pepper. Add drained, soaked raisins. Cover and blend at high speed until smooth and creamy. If necessary, add 1 tablespoon water in which raisins were soaked (or water) to make a good dipping consistency. Serve well chilled with a selection of vegetables, such as cauliflowerets, carrot sticks, blanched green beans, radish roses, broccoli, celery sticks, zucchini sticks, or cooked artichokes.

Raisin-Cream Cheese Spread   1 1/4 cups

Try this tangy cheese spread on thin slices of pumpernickel or crisp rounds of melba toast for a new and imaginative appetizer.

1 package (8 ounces) cream
   cheese, at room temperature
1/3 cup Sun-Maid® Seedless
   Raisins or Currants
1/2 teaspoon ginger

1/4 teaspoon salt
2 tablespoons chutney,
   chopped
4 to 5 tablespoons
   medium-dry sherry

Beat the cream cheese until smooth; then work in the raisins, ginger, salt, and chutney. Add the sherry, a tablespoon at a time, until the mixture is of spreading consistency.

Appetizer Egg Rolls   24 appetizers

Almost American by adoption, egg rolls are given a new dimension with the addition of tiny, tart currants.

1/2 pound boneless pork,
   cut into julienne
1 small onion, sliced
1 cup shredded Chinese
   or green cabbage
2 tablespoons vegetable oil
1/2 cup sliced mushrooms
1/4 cup bean or alfalfa
   sprouts
1/4 cup Sun-Maid® Zante
   Currants

1/4 cup slivered almonds
1 teaspoon cornstarch
2 tablespoons dry sherry
1 tablespoon soy sauce
1/2 teaspoon ginger
12 egg roll wrappers
   (about 6 inches square)
   Oil for deep-fat frying
   Ginger Apricot Sauce
   (page 122)

Sauté the pork, onion, and cabbage in hot oil until lightly browned. Stir in the mushrooms, bean sprouts, currants, and almonds and sauté, stirring, for 1 minute. Dissolve the cornstarch in 2 tablespoons water and combine with the sherry, soy sauce, and ginger; add to the pork mixture and bring to a boil, stirring. Remove from heat and cool.

Stack the egg roll wrappers and cut in half to form rectangles. Forming one roll at a time, place a heaping teaspoonful of pork mixture on one end of a rectangle, moisten the long edges, and roll up. Press the edges together to seal.

Egg rolls may be prepared to this point, then refrigerated for several hours or overnight or frozen for several days before frying. Adjust time for browning. If rolls are frozen, let them thaw before cooking.

Heat the oil to 375° F and fry the egg rolls, 4 or 5 at a time, until golden brown and crisp on all sides. Frying will take about 4 or 5 minutes; turn rolls once. Drain on paper towels and keep warm while frying the remaining rolls. Serve with warm Ginger Apricot Sauce.

Appetizer Cheese Ball

12 servings

A cheese ball dresses up any party, particularly if the parsley-green ball is surrounded by golden and red apple wedges.

1 package (8 ounces) cream cheese at room temperature
4 ounces blue cheese, crumbled
1 cup (4 ounces) shredded Cheddar cheese
2 teaspoons Dijon-style mustard
1 teaspoon Worcestershire sauce
1/8 teaspoon garlic powder
1/4 teaspoon salt
1/2 cup finely chopped pecans
2/3 cup Sun-Maid® Zante Currants
3/4 cup (about) chopped parsley
Assorted crackers
Apple wedges

Place the cream cheese, blue cheese, Cheddar cheese, mustard, Worcestershire, garlic powder, and salt in a mixer bowl and beat at low speed just until well mixed. Stir in the pecans and currants. Taste and adjust seasoning. Refrigerate the cheese mixture for 30 minutes, or until slightly firm, then shape into a ball. Roll in the chopped parsley to coat well. Cover with plastic wrap and refrigerate until ready to serve. Let stand at room temperature for about 30 minutes before serving. Place on a platter surrounded with crackers and apple wedges.

Shrimp and Avocado Appetizers

4 to 6 servings

Hot shrimp in a spicy sauce contrast with the cool smoothness of avocado. Serve this appetizer at the beginning of an otherwise light meal.

1/2 pound small shrimp, thawed if frozen, shelled and deveined
3 tablespoons vegetable oil
1 large onion, chopped
1 clove garlic, minced
2 large tomatoes, peeled and diced
1/2 cup Sun-Maid® Seedless Golden Raisins
1 tablespoon white vinegar
1 teaspoon ginger
1/2 teaspoon turmeric
1/4 teaspoon cumin
1/4 teaspoon hot pepper sauce
1/2 teaspoon salt
1 large avocado
Lemon juice

Sauté the shrimp in hot oil just until they turn pink. Remove from the oil with a slotted spoon. Add the onion and garlic and sauté until the onion is soft but not browned. Stir in the tomatoes, raisins, vinegar, ginger, turmeric, cumin, hot pepper sauce, and salt and bring to a boil. Reduce heat, cover, and simmer for 10 minutes.

Meanwhile, peel and pit the avocado; cut into quarters or sixths, depending on the number of servings. Brush each wedge lightly with lemon juice, sprinkle with salt, and arrange on a serving dish. Drain any liquid that may have collected on the shrimp and add the shrimp to the tomato mixture. Cook for 1 to 2 minutes to heat. Spoon the shrimp and sauce over the avocado wedges and serve immediately.

Seviche with Avocado   6 servings

In this famous fish dish, the lemon juice actually "cooks" the fish. You can also serve the fish with picks as a cocktail tidbit.

1 pound scallops or
    white fish fillets
3/4 cup lime or lemon juice
1/3 cup Sun-Maid® Seedless
    Raisins
1 medium-size onion, minced
1 medium-size tomato,
    minced

4 tablespoons chopped
    parsley, divided
2 tablespoons olive oil
1/2 teaspoon salt
1/4 teaspoon crushed red
    pepper
3 avocados, peeled and
    halved lengthwise

Cut the scallops or fish into small, thin slices and combine with the lime juice. Cover and refrigerate for 2 to 4 hours. Gently fold in the raisins, onion, tomato, 2 tablespoons of the parsley, oil, salt, and crushed red pepper. Return to the refrigerator to chill. Spoon into the avocado halves. Garnish with remaining chopped parsley.

Pork Satay   6 to 8 servings

An exotic apricot-peanut butter dipping sauce makes these appetizer kabobs unforgettable. Indonesian bliss!

1/2 pound lean boneless pork
2 tablespoons soy sauce
2 tablespoons thick steak
    sauce
10 dried apricots

1/4 cup creamy or chunky
    peanut butter
1/2 teaspoon salt
5 drops hot pepper sauce

Cut the pork into 3/4-inch cubes and combine with the soy sauce and steak sauce. Cover and refrigerate for several hours, stirring occasionally.

Meanwhile, simmer the apricots in 3/4 cup water for 5 minutes. Place apricots and their cooking liquid in a blender container or food processor. Add peanut butter, salt, and hot pepper sauce. Cover and process until smooth. Reheat when ready to serve. Thread the marinated pork cubes on skewers. (If you use wooden skewers, soak them in water 2 hours before using.) Brush with any remaining soy sauce mixture. Cook over hot coals or under broiler for 6 to 8 minutes, turning often. Serve with the warm apricot-peanut butter sauce for dipping.

Satay serves 2 when served as a main course. Double the meat portion of the recipe for 4 people.

If you like, serve kabobs of mushrooms along with the pork. Thread small fresh mushrooms on separate skewers, brush with melted butter, and grill or broil along with the pork.

Opposite: Pork Satay with Apricot Dipping Sauce, Edam-Shrimp Appetizer (page 16), Seviche with Avocado

Edam-Shrimp Appetizer   4 to 8 servings

A sensational appetizer that can double as a luncheon or even a dinner entrée. When served as a main course, it needs only a tossed salad and thin pumpernickel bread to accompany it.

1 15-ounce Edam cheese, divided
1/2 pound shrimp, thawed if
    frozen, shelled and deveined
1/4 cup minced onion
2 tablespoons butter or
    margarine
1 medium-size tomato,
    finely chopped
1 cup fresh bread crumbs
1/3 cup Sun-Maid® Seedless
    Raisins

2 tablespoons capers or
    chopped pimiento-
    stuffed green olives
1/4 teaspoon salt
1/8 teaspoon freshly
    ground pepper
1 egg, lightly beaten
1 slice lemon
Watercress

Grease a 1-quart soufflé dish or straight-sided casserole. Remove wax coating from cheese. Cut into 1/4-inch slices. Use about 2/3 of the slices to line the bottom and sides of the baking dish. Dice the remaining cheese and set aside.

Reserve 1 or 2 shrimp for garnish. Finely dice the remaining shrimp. Preheat the oven to 350° F. Sauté diced shrimp, whole shrimp, and onion in butter until shrimp turn pink. Reserve the whole shrimp. Stir in 1/2 cup of the diced cheese, the tomato, bread crumbs, raisins, capers, salt, pepper, and egg. Spoon into cheese-lined baking dish. Sprinkle remaining diced cheese over shrimp mixture in dish. Bake in preheated oven 30 minutes. Let stand 15 to 20 minutes in dish. Invert onto a platter. Garnish top with the whole shrimp, lemon slice, and watercress. To serve, cut into wedges.

Note: When lining the baking dish with cheese, don't worry about a perfect fit; the cheese melts and fills any holes during baking.

Wine Fruit Cup   6 servings

Lovely to look at and delicate in flavor, this fruit cup can easily double as a dessert.

1 1/2 cups dry white wine
1/2 cup sugar
1 tablespoon lemon juice
1 1/2 teaspoons anise seed
1/4 teaspoon salt

1 small stick cinnamon
1/2 cup Sun-Maid® Seedless
    Golden Raisins
4 purple plums, sliced
2 nectarines, sliced

In an enameled or stainless steel saucepan, combine the wine, sugar, lemon juice, anise seed, salt, and cinnamon stick and bring to a boil. Turn off heat and cool to room temperature.

Combine the raisins, plums, and peaches in a bowl and strain the cooled wine syrup over them. Cover and refrigerate for several hours, stirring occasionally.

Dolmathes

30 appetizers

Stuffed grape leaves, a Greek appetizer, are easy on the hostess. Make them the day before and serve chilled.

2 large onions, finely
  chopped
1 clove garlic, minced
1/3 cup olive oil
1/2 cup long-grained rice
1/2 cup Sun-Maid® Zante
  Currants
1/2 cup pine nuts or
  slivered almonds
1 teaspoon salt
1/4 teaspoon freshly
  ground black pepper

3/4 cup lemon juice,
  divided
4 tablespoons chopped
  fresh dill or 2 1/2
  teaspoons dried
  dillweed, divided
1 jar (7 to 9 ounces)
  grape leaves in brine
1 cup plain yogurt

Sauté the onions and garlic in oil until the onion is soft but not browned. Add the rice and cook, stirring, 5 minutes longer. Add 1 1/4 cups water, the currants, pine nuts, salt, pepper, 1/4 cup of the lemon juice, and 3 tablespoons of the fresh dill or 2 teaspoons of the dillweed; bring to a boil. Reduce heat, cover, and simmer for 15 minutes. Remove from heat and cool until easy to handle.

Rinse the grape leaves in cold water and separate. Place the leaves shiny-side down on a work surface, using the whole large leaves or overlapping 2 smaller leaves. With larger leaves, use a sharp knife to remove the heavy stem and vein. Spoon 1 tablespoon rice mixture onto each leaf near the stem. Fold the sides of the leaves over the filling, then starting with the stem end, roll toward the point. Place point down in a 10- to 12-inch skillet. Arrange all the packets close together in one skillet, making 2 layers if necessary.

Add the remaining 1/2 cup lemon juice and 1 cup water to the skillet. Place a heavy plate on top of the stuffed leaves (an 8- or 9-inch pie plate is perfect in some skillets; half fill with water for extra weight). Gently bring to a boil. Reduce heat to low, cover, and simmer for 30 minutes. Remove the skillet from the heat and allow the stuffed leaves to cool in their cooking liquid.

Before serving, combine the yogurt with the remaining 1 tablespoon of fresh dill or the 1/2 teaspoon of dillweed. (If desired, season with salt, pepper, and lemon juice.) To serve, arrange 3 or 4 dolmathes on small appetizer plates. Top with a dollop of the dilled yogurt.

Buttermilk and Beet Soup   6 servings

This chilled soup is as pretty to look at as it is good to eat.

1 small onion, chopped
2 tablespoons butter or
   margarine
1 cup shrimp, thawed if
   frozen, shelled and
   deveined
3 cups buttermilk
1 can (8 ounces) julienne beets,
   drained

1/2 cup Sun-Maid® Zante
   Currants
1 tablespoon fresh dill,
   chopped, or 1 teaspoon
   dried dillweed
1/4 teaspoon salt
Dill sprigs

Sauté the onion in butter until soft but not browned. Coarsely chop the shrimp, add to the onion in the pan and sauté, stirring, until they turn pink; cool. Combine the shrimp mixture in a large bowl with the buttermilk, beets, currants, dill, and salt. Cover and refrigerate until well chilled. Serve in soup bowls, garnished with dill sprigs.

Raisin Peanut Soup   4 to 6 servings

This is a rich and very satisfying soup best served with a light entrée.

1 can (10 3/4 ounces)
   condensed chicken broth,
   undiluted
1 soup can half-and-half
   or milk
1/2 cup creamy or chunky
   peanut butter
1/3 cup Sun-Maid® Seedless
   Golden Raisins, chopped

1/8 teaspoon salt
5 to 10 drops hot
   pepper sauce
1 tablespoon medium-dry
   sherry
Sliced scallions

Heat the chicken broth with the half-and-half until bubbles form around the edges of the saucepan. Add the peanut butter, whisking until smooth, then stir in the remaining ingredients except scallions. Serve warm or chilled. Garnish with sliced scallions.

Cold Fruit Soup   8 servings

Icy-cold fruit soups are Scandinavia's contribution to good eating. They are an ideal brunch appetizer and make a delicious dessert as well.

1 can (6 ounces) frozen
   lemonade concentrate
1 can (12 ounces) apricot
   nectar
1/2 cup dried apricots, halved
1/3 cup Sun-Maid® Seedless
   Raisins
2 tablespoons sugar

1 3-inch stick cinnamon
3 whole allspice or cloves
2 tablespoons cornstarch
1 bag (20 ounces) frozen
   mixed fruit,
   partially thawed
Dairy sour cream

Mix the lemonade concentrate with 2 cans of water in a 3-quart saucepan. Add the apricot nectar, apricots, raisins, sugar, cinnamon, and allspice. Bring to a boil, stirring once. Reduce heat and simmer, uncovered, for 5 minutes. Dissolve the cornstarch in 2 tablespoons cold water and stir into the soup; cook until the mixture boils and thickens. Remove from the heat and cool for 15 minutes before stirring in the frozen fruit. Refrigerate until well chilled. Serve with dollop of sour cream.

Herring Salad   6 servings

For a handsome presentation, serve this salad on a lettuce-lined platter, garnished with sliced hard-cooked eggs and apples.

1 jar (12 ounces) pickled herring in wine sauce, drained	1/4 cup Sun-Maid® Zante Currants
2 medium-size cooked potatoes, coarsely chopped	2 tablespoons capers
	1/4 teaspoon salt
	Dash freshly ground pepper
3/4 cup pickled beets, coarsely chopped	1/4 cup white wine vinegar
1 small onion, minced	1/2 cup dairy sour cream, optional

Cut the herring into 1-inch pieces and combine with the remaining ingredients, tossing lightly to mix. Cover and refrigerate for 2 to 3 hours to blend the flavors.

Serve with chewy, dark pumpernickel bread for a great flavor contrast.

Gazpacho   4 to 6 servings

Currants give this popular chilled soup a new taste.

3 large ripe tomatoes, peeled, seeded, and coarsely diced	3/4 teaspoon salt
1/2 small onion, cut up	1 large cucumber, peeled
1 clove garlic	1 large green pepper, seeded and diced
1/4 teaspoon cumin	1/3 cup Sun-Maid® Zante Currants
1/4 cup white wine vinegar or lemon juice	Croutons
3 tablespoons olive oil	

Place the tomatoes, onion, garlic, cumin, vinegar, olive oil, salt, and 1/2 cup water in a blender container or food processor and process until smooth. Cut the cucumber in half lengthwise and scoop out the seeds with the tip of a spoon. Cut the cucumber into chunks and add to the blender container with the green pepper. Turn blender on and off quickly to coarsely chop the cucumber and pepper. Add the currants and process just to mix. Correct the seasoning. Chill well before serving. Serve in chilled bowls garnished with croutons.

Curried Yogurt Soup

6 servings

This attractively-colored soup is a good opener for an important dinner.

1 cup chopped carrots
1 medium-size onion,
    chopped
1 teaspoon curry powder
1/4 cup butter or margarine
1/3 cup Sun-Maid® Seedless
    Golden Raisins

1/2 teaspoon salt
1 can (10 3/4 ounces)
    condensed chicken
    broth, undiluted
2 cups plain yogurt, at
    room temperature
Shredded cucumber

Sauté the carrots, onion, and curry powder in butter until the onion is soft but not browned. Stir in raisins, salt, and chicken broth and bring to a boil. Reduce heat, cover, and simmer for 10 minutes. Pour carrot mixture into a blender container or food processor and process until smooth. Add the yogurt and process just until mixed. Pour into individual bowls and serve immediately garnished with shredded cucumber. (This soup is best eaten at the temperature it ends up — warm.)

Caponata

8 to 10 servings

This dish is so good that it's sometimes called "eggplant caviar."

2 medium-size eggplants
4 teaspoons salt, divided
1 cup olive oil, divided
1 large onion, chopped
1/2 cup minced celery
1 clove garlic, minced
1 can (8 ounces) tomato sauce
    or 1 1/2 cups chopped,
    peeled tomatoes (preferably
    Italian plum tomatoes)

1/3 cup red wine vinegar
1/3 cup Sun-Maid® Zante
    Currants
2 tablespoons chopped
    dill pickle
1 tablespoon capers
Freshly ground pepper
Crusty Italian bread
    slices

Peel the eggplants and cut into 1/2-inch dice (there should be about 8 cups). Sprinkle with 3 teaspoons of the salt and toss to mix. Place in a colander and let drain for about 1 hour. Rinse the eggplant and dry well on paper towels.

Heat 2/3 cup of the olive oil in a large skillet. Add the eggplant and sauté slowly until lightly browned; remove from skillet. Add the remaining 1/3 cup oil to skillet and heat. Add the onion, celery, and garlic and cook until the onion is soft but not browned. Add the tomato sauce, cover, and simmer for 10 minutes, stirring frequently. Return the eggplant to the skillet and stir in the vinegar, currants, pickle, and capers. Add the remaining 1 teaspoon salt and pepper to taste. Cover and simmer for 15 to 20 minutes, or until thick and dark; stir frequently. Chill well before serving, surrounded with Italian bread slices.

Hot and Hearty
Main Dishes for
Memorable Meals

There's solid goodness in these fruit-studded main dishes sure to please family and guests alike. Some are fancy; some are homey. Every one of them will add something special to your menus.

Skillet Apricot Chicken   4 servings

There's a hint of the Orient in this easy and elegant way of cooking chicken. Natural sun-ripened dried apricots provide the tart-sweet sauce.

> 1 (3-pound) broiler-fryer, cut up
> 2 tablespoons all-purpose flour
> 3/4 teaspoon garlic powder
> 1/2 teaspoon salt
> 1/4 teaspoon ginger
> 1 tablespoon vegetable oil
> 3/4 cup orange juice
> 1/4 cup honey
> 2 chicken bouillon cubes, crumbled
> 1/2 teaspoon rosemary, crushed
> 1 (3-inch) stick cinnamon
> 1/2 cup dried apricots
> 1/2 cup sliced scallions

Wash and dry the chicken. Mix the flour, garlic powder, salt, and ginger. Roll chicken pieces in the flour mixture. Heat the oil in a large skillet and add the chicken. Sauté until browned on both sides. Combine the juice, honey, bouillon, and rosemary. Pour over the chicken. Add the cinnamon stick, apricots, and scallions. Heat to boiling. Reduce heat, cover, and simmer for 25 minutes. Uncover and cook over medium heat 3 to 5 minutes, spooning sauce over chicken frequently until chicken is glazed.

Mexican Chicken Olé

4 servings

Olé means "wow" and that's what this recipe is. It's quick, easy, raisin-rich, and thrifty.

1 3-pound broiler-fryer, cut up
Salt and freshly ground
  pepper
2 tablespoons vegetable oil
1/2 cup Sun-Maid® Seedless
  Raisins
1 medium-size onion, thinly
  sliced
1 clove garlic, minced

1/4 teaspoon thyme
1 can (8 ounces) stewed
  tomatoes
1 can (7 ounces) chopped
  green chilies
1/4 cup dry white wine or
  dry vermouth
Chopped parsley

Lightly sprinkle the chicken with salt and pepper and brown on both sides in oil in a large skillet. Add the raisins, onion, garlic, and thyme. Reduce heat, cover, and simmer for 5 minutes. Add the tomatoes, chilies, and wine and bring to a boil. Reduce heat, cover, and simmer for 25 minutes. Serve on a warmed platter, sprinkled with parsley.

Accompany this Mexican chicken with hot tortillas, steaming rice, and a chilled salad. Make your favorite chocolate concoction for dessert. "Olé!"

Coconut Chicken

4 servings

A feast for the eyes and the palate, this spicy, red-brown tomato sauce is offset by cream-colored shreds of subtly-flavored coconut.

1/2 teaspoon turmeric
1/2 teaspoon ginger
1/2 teaspoon cumin
2 teaspoons salt
1 3-pound broiler-fryer,
  cut up
1/4 cup butter or margarine
2 medium-size onions,
  chopped
2 cloves garlic, minced
3 medium-size tomatoes,
  seeded and chopped

1/2 cup Sun-Maid® Seedless
  Raisins
Juice of 1 lemon
2 teaspoons coriander
1/2 teaspoon cayenne
1/4 teaspoon cinnamon
1/4 teaspoon cardamom or
  4 whole cardamom seeds
1 cup shredded coconut,
  divided

Combine the turmeric, ginger, cumin, and salt and sprinkle the mixture over the chicken, rubbing it into the skin. Melt the butter in a large skillet. Add the chicken and brown on both sides; remove from skillet and reserve. Add the onions and garlic and sauté for 1 minute. Stir in the tomatoes, raisins, and lemon juice and return the chicken to the skillet. Sprinkle with the remaining spices. Cover and simmer for 40 minutes, spooning the sauce over the chicken two or three times. Remove the chicken to a warmed platter. Stir 1/2 cup of the coconut into the sauce. Spoon the sauce over the chicken and sprinkle with the remaining 1/2 cup coconut.

Serve the chicken with hot rice and bowls of yogurt, chopped cucumbers, chopped peanuts, banana chips, and kumquats from which diners can help themselves. A watercress salad and a simple fruit dessert complete an out-of-this-world dinner.

Chicken and Peanut Stew   4 servings

This unusual and delicious chicken stew is of African origin. So is the okra, or gombo, cooked with it.

1/4 cup all-purpose flour
2 teaspoons salt
2 teaspoons ginger
1 3-pound broiler-fryer,
   cut up
1/4 cup vegetable oil
1 large onion, chopped
2 cloves garlic, minced
1 can (16 ounces) whole
   tomatoes
3/4 cup Sun-Maid® Seedless
   Raisins
1/4 cup peanut butter
1/4 to 1 teaspoon hot
   pepper sauce
1 package (10 ounces)
   frozen okra, thawed
Hot, cooked rice

Garnishes:
mixture of dark and
   golden raisins
shredded coconut and
   crushed pineapple
diced tomato and avocado
Onion-Raisin Relish
   (page 61)
Dried-Fruit Chutney
   (page 64)

Combine the flour, salt, and ginger and coat the chicken. Heat the oil in a large skillet and sauté the chicken until browned on both sides; remove from the skillet and set aside. Add the onion and garlic to the skillet and sauté, stirring, until the onion is soft but not browned. Stir in the tomatoes, raisins, peanut butter, hot pepper sauce, and 1 cup water. Cook, stirring until the peanut butter melts. Return the chicken to skillet, basting it with the sauce; top with the okra. Cover and simmer for 40 minutes, or until the chicken is tender, turning the pieces once or twice with tongs. Serve surrounded with rice and a selection of garnishes.

Place each garnish in a separate serving bowl and pass at the table. A cold lemon soufflé would make a refreshing dessert.

Pineapple Chicken

6 servings

Rosemary and raisins add a subtle and haunting flavor to this easily made casserole.

3 whole chicken breasts,
    halved, or 6 chicken legs
    (drumstick and thigh)
3 tablespoons vegetable oil
1 large onion, chopped
1 clove garlic, minced
3 large tomatoes, seeded
    and chopped, or 1 can
    (16 ounces) whole
    tomatoes, drained and
    chopped

1/2 cup Sun-Maid® Seedless
    Golden Raisins
2 tablespoons lemon juice
1 teaspoon rosemary,
    crumbled
1 1/2 teaspoons salt
1 can (8 ounces)
    crushed pineapple

In a large skillet, brown the chicken in oil on all sides; remove and set aside. Add the onion and garlic to the skillet and sauté until the onion is soft but not browned. Add the remaining ingredients, except the pineapple, and bring to a boil. Return the chicken to the skillet, basting with the sauce. Reduce heat, cover, and simmer for 40 minutes, or until the chicken is fork-tender. Arrange the chicken pieces on a warmed serving platter. Add the pineapple to the tomato sauce and heat, stirring. Spoon the sauce over the chicken and serve immediately.

Consider serving this dish with parsleyed rice, preceded by a California-style salad of grapefruit and avocado. Add wine and a molded dessert and you're set to entertain.

Currant Turkey 'Burgers

4 servings

A juicy, low-calorie answer for 'burger lovers who have to watch their weight.

1 pound ground turkey
1/2 cup fresh bread crumbs
1/3 cup Sun-Maid® Zante
    Currants

1 small onion, minced
1 teaspoon salt
1/8 teaspoon freshly ground
    pepper

Combine all ingredients with 1/4 cup water and mix well with your hands until smooth. Shape the mixture into 4-inch patties and place on a greased rack in the broiler pan. Broil 5 inches from the heat for about 6 minutes on each side. These are excellent served on toasted English muffins.

Variation

Hawaiian: Add 1/4 cup minced green pepper with the other ingredients. Omit water, adding 1/4 cup pineapple juice or 1/4 cup crushed pineapple instead.

Opposite: Chicken and Peanut Stew (page 23)

Chicken and Bulgur Stew   6 servings

This hearty raisin-enriched chicken stew is thickened with bulgur, a parched cracked wheat favored by the Turks.

2 large onions, chopped
1/3 cup butter or margarine
1/2 cup Sun-Maid® Puffed
    Seeded Muscat Raisins
1 cup bulgur
1/2 teaspoon cardamom or
    cinnamon

2 1/2 teaspoons salt
1 teaspoon freshly ground
    pepper
1 3-pound broiler-fryer,
    quartered

In a dutch oven, sauté the onions in the butter until lightly browned. Add 6 cups water and the raisins, bulgur, cardamom, salt, and pepper, stirring until smooth. Add the chicken and bring to a boil. Reduce heat, cover, and simmer for 1 hour, stirring occasionally. Remove the chicken from the sauce and let stand until cool enough to handle. Cut the meat into bite-size pieces, discarding the skin and bones, and return to the dutch oven. Simmer just until heated through.

Serve in soup bowls, with a tomato salad, corn bread, or Boston Brown Bread (page 77), and sherbet.

Stir-Fried Chicken Hawaiian   4 servings

Successful stir-frying requires that all the ingredients be ready before you start cooking. Once everything is properly organized, the actual cooking can be done in just a few minutes.

2 whole chicken breasts,
    skinned and boned
1 medium-size onion
1 tablespoon cornstarch
1/2 teaspoon ginger
1/2 teaspoon salt
1/8 teaspoon freshly ground
    pepper
1 can (8 ounces) pineapple
    slices, halved
3 tablespoons soy sauce
5 tablespoons vegetable
    oil, divided

2 cups shredded Chinese
    or green cabbage
2 ribs celery,
    thinly sliced
1/2 cup Sun-Maid®
    Seedless Golden Raisins
1/4 cup macadamia nuts,
    chopped
1 can (7 ounces) water
    chestnuts, thinly sliced
Hot, cooked rice

Cut the chicken breasts crosswise into 1/4-inch slices and the onion into very thin wedges. Set both aside. Combine the cornstarch, ginger, salt, and pepper with 1/4 cup water in a small bowl. Drain the juice from the pineapple into the bowl and stir in the soy sauce. Reserve the pineapple.

Heat 2 tablespoons of the oil in a wok or large skillet. Add the cabbage and celery and cook over very high heat; stir quickly and constantly (stir-fry) until tender-crisp, about 2 to 3 minutes. Remove the cabbage mixture from the pan and reserve. Add the remaining 3 tablespoons oil. Add the chicken and onion and stir-fry until the chicken is opaque. Reduce heat and blend in the cornstarch mixture. Cook until thickened, then add the pineapple, raisins, nuts, and water chestnuts. Cover and simmer 5 minutes. Stir in the reserved cabbage mixture. Toss to mix and heat through. Serve immediately on a bed of cooked rice.

This dish merits sharing with friends. Start with Appetizer Egg Rolls (page 12) and end with iced melon and, of course, fortune cookies.

Chicken in Cider   4 servings

Raisins and hot Italian sausage provide the seasoning for this flavorful chicken dish, while red apple wedges make a cheery and healthful garnish.

1 3-pound broiler-fryer,	*3/4 cup Sun-Maid® Seedless*
cut up	*Raisins*
1/4 pound (2 or 3) hot Italian	*1 1/2 teaspoons salt*
sausages, halved crosswise	*1 tablespoon cornstarch*
2 tablespoons vegetable oil	*Red apple wedges*
1 large onion, chopped	*Parsley or watercress*
1 1/2 cups apple cider or juice	

In a large skillet, sauté the chicken and sausages in hot oil until lightly browned; remove from the skillet with a slotted spoon and pour off all but 2 tablespoons of the fat. Add the onion and sauté until soft but not browned. Stir in the cider, raisins, and salt and return the chicken and sausages to the skillet, spooning the sauce over them. Cover and simmer for 30 minutes, turning the chicken once. Remove chicken and sausages to a warmed serving platter. Blend the cornstarch with 2 tablespoons water and add to the sauce. Bring to a boil, stirring constantly. Spoon the sauce over the chicken and serve garnished with apple wedges and parsley or watercress.

Mini Meat Loaves
6 servings

Small meat loaves cook quickly and add an individual touch to your dinner table. Currants, soy sauce, and ginger make this entrée even more appealing.

1 1/2 pounds lean ground beef
1 cup fresh bread crumbs
1/2 cup Sun-Maid® Zante
    Currants
1 small onion, minced
3 tablespoons soy sauce
1/2 teaspoon ginger

1/2 teaspoon salt
2 eggs
1 cup sliced scallions
    (including lots of
    the green)

Preheat the oven to 375° F. Place all the ingredients except the scallions in a large bowl. Add 1/2 cup water and mix with your hands until the mixture is very smooth. Shape into six small, oval loaves. Place in 13×9×2-inch baking pan. You may brush the loaves with additional soy sauce. Bake for 30 minutes. Remove the loaves from the pan with a slotted pancake turner and drain briefly on paper towels before placing on a warmed platter. Garnish loaves with sliced scallions.

Mini meat loaves would team well with rice and a stir-fry of Chinese vegetables.

Jambalaya
4 servings

Jambalaya, a ham and seafood dish created in the Creole kitchens of New Orleans, is full of wonderful flavors.

1 medium-size onion, chopped
1 medium-size green pepper,
    seeded and chopped
2 ribs celery, chopped
2 tablespoons vegetable oil
1 cup diced smoked ham or
    1/2 cup crisply fried,
    crumbled bacon
3 cups chicken broth
1 can (8 ounces) tomato sauce
1 teaspoon thyme
1 cup long-grained rice

Salt and freshly ground
    pepper
12 clams in shell or 1 can
    (10 ounces) whole baby
    clams, undrained
1 pound haddock, cod, or
    turbot fillets or shrimp,
    thawed if frozen,
    shelled and deveined
1/2 cup Sun-Maid® Puffed
    Seeded Muscat Raisins
Parsley sprigs

In a dutch oven, sauté the onion, green pepper, and celery in oil until the onion is tender but not browned. Add the ham, chicken broth, tomato sauce, thyme, rice, and salt and pepper to taste and bring to a boil. Reduce heat, cover, and simmer for 10 to 15 minutes, or until the rice is nearly tender.

Meanwhile, scrub the clams well and cut the fish into 1-inch cubes. Add fish and raisins to the rice mixture and stir lightly to combine. Top with the clams in shell, cover, and simmer 5 minutes, or until fish flakes easily with a fork and the clam shells open; discard any clams that do not open. (If using canned clams, add them at this point; stir very gently and heat 1 to 2 minutes.) Spoon the rice mixture into a large shallow bowl and garnish with the clams and parsley sprigs.

Serve jambalaya with Southern-style biscuits, plenty of butter, and a green salad. Watermelon ice would be a cooling and light close to this rich repast.

Imperial Fish Casserole   4 servings

A tangy custard conceals tender fish and sherry-scented currants in a dish fit for imperial palates.

1/3 up Sun-Maid® Zante Currants	1/2 teaspoon salt
	1/8 teaspoon cayenne
3 tablespoons medium-dry sherry	1 1/2 cups half-and-half or light cream
1 pound haddock or white fish fillets	2 eggs, lightly beaten
	2 slices bread, cubed
3 tablespoons butter or margarine	1/4 cup chopped parsley
	2 tablespoons minced onion
3 tablespoons all-purpose flour	Paprika
	Melted butter
1/4 teaspoon nutmeg	

Grease a 1 1/2-quart casserole. Combine the currants and sherry in a small bowl and let stand for at least 20 minutes. Bring 2 cups water to a boil in a large skillet and add the fish. Reduce heat, cover, and simmer for 3 to 5 minutes or just until the fish flakes easily with a fork. Using a slotted spatula, carefully remove the fish from the pan; drain well, flake, and set aside.

Melt the 3 tablespoons butter in a saucepan. Add the flour, nutmeg, salt, and cayenne, and cook, stirring until the mixture bubbles. Gradually blend in the half-and-half, continuing to stir until the sauce thickens. Remove from heat and slowly whisk some of the hot sauce into the beaten eggs. Return the egg mixture to the saucepan, whisking until smooth.

Preheat the oven to 375°F. Combine the bread cubes, parsley, onion, and sherried currants with the sauce and gently fold in the flaked fish. Spoon the mixture into the prepared casserole and sprinkle with paprika. Bake for 25 to 30 minutes, or until golden brown and set in the center. Remove from the oven and let stand for 10 minutes before serving. Pass melted butter to spoon over the custard.

Accompany this dish with a rice and vegetable pilaf and broiled tomatoes for color. Pear halves sprinkled with chopped walnuts and kirsch would make a lovely dessert.

Baked Fish Fillets Mediterranean   4 servings

An easy and flavorful way to prepare fish fillets. Buttery bread crumbs, raisins, and cheese are combined for the filling. Tangy mustard is used for the finishing touch.

3/4 cup fresh bread crumbs, divided
1/3 cup Sun-Maid® Seedless Raisins
1/4 cup chopped parsley
1/4 cup grated Parmesan cheese
3 tablespoons butter or margarine, melted
4 white fish fillets (6 to 8 ounces each) (red snapper, cod, haddock, flounder)

Salt and freshly ground pepper
Prepared mustard
Lemon wedges
Parsley sprigs

Preheat oven to 400°F. Combine 1/2 cup of the bread crumbs, raisins, chopped parsley, and cheese. Add melted butter. Toss. Sprinkle fish lightly with salt and pepper. Spoon about 1/4 cup of filling onto fish. Fold in the ends of the fish and roll. Place seam side down in lightly greased baking dish. Spread the top of each roll with 1 teaspoon mustard. Sprinkle with remaining bread crumbs. Bake for 20 minutes or until fish flakes easily. Serve with lemon wedges and parsley sprigs.

Meat Loaf Parmesan   6 to 8 servings

A speedy meat loaf with texture and tang that's easy to prepare for a weekday dinner.

1 1/2 pounds lean ground beef
1 cup rolled oats
1 cup tomato juice
1/2 cup Sun-Maid® Seedless Raisins
1/4 cup minced onion
1/4 cup grated Parmesan cheese

1 egg
1 teaspoon oregano
1 1/2 teaspoons salt
1/4 teaspoon freshly ground pepper
1 large tomato, sliced
Tomato sauce

Preheat the oven to 350°F. Place all the ingredients except the tomatoes in a large bowl and mix with your hands until very smooth. Shape the mixture into an 8×4-inch oval and place in a 13×9×2-inch baking pan, overlapping the tomato slices on top of the loaf. Bake for 1 hour; remove from the oven and let stand 5 minutes before placing on a warmed serving platter.

Slice the meat loaf and serve it with tomato sauce and additional grated Parmesan cheese.

Round out the menu with noodles and buttered broccoli.

Mache Qorma
4 servings

Flounder fillets in a rose-colored sauce — a dish of Indonesian origin to serve when company is coming.

4 large fillets of flounder
  (1 to 1 1/2 pounds)
  Salt and freshly ground
  pepper
1/4 cup vegetable oil
2 medium-size onions, sliced
1 clove garlic, minced
1/2 cup tomato juice
1/3 cup Sun-Maid® Seedless
  Raisins

2 teaspoons curry powder
1/2 teaspoon cumin
1/8 to 1/4 teaspoon cayenne
  pepper
1 cup plain yogurt, at
  room temperature
1/4 cup sliced almonds,
  toasted

Pat the fish dry with paper towels and lightly sprinkle with salt and pepper. Heat the oil in a large skillet and brown the fish on both sides; remove the fish and keep warm. Sauté the onions and garlic in the oil until the onions are soft but not browned. Add the tomato juice, raisins, and seasonings and bring to a boil. Reduce heat and simmer for 2 to 3 minutes. Stir in the yogurt and return the fish to the skillet, basting with the sauce. Simmer for 2 to 3 minutes, or until the fish is heated through. Sprinkle with the almonds and serve immediately.

This dish is delightful with a rice pilaf and a tossed salad. Serve sliced oranges topped with freshly grated coconut for dessert.

Fruited Pork Stew
4 servings

This rich-flavored stew, redolent of apples, apricots, and prunes, is proof-positive of pork's affinity for fruit.

1 pound boneless pork for
  stewing, cut into
  1-inch cubes
2 small onions, quartered
1 tablespoon vegetable oil
1 cup chicken broth
1 teaspoon salt
1/4 teaspoon freshly ground
  pepper

1/4 teaspoon ginger
1/4 cup dried apricots
1/2 cup pitted prunes
1 large cooking apple,
  cut into 1-inch chunks
Hot, cooked noodles

In a dutch oven, sauté the pork cubes and onions in oil until browned. Add the chicken broth, salt, pepper, and ginger, stirring to combine, and bring to a boil. Reduce heat, cover, and simmer for 30 minutes. Add the apricots, prunes, and apple and simmer, covered, 20 minutes longer, or until the pork is fork-tender. Serve the stew in a deep platter, surrounded with noodles.

A tossed salad of sliced, raw zucchini and romaine lettuce would be a refreshing follow-up for this rich pork stew.

Burritos

6 servings

Another delicious way of serving beef with beans and tortillas from south of the border. Serve with a crisp green salad and fresh fruit for dessert.

2 large green peppers, seeded and diced
1 large onion, chopped
1/2 cup vegetable oil, divided
1 pound lean ground beef
1 can (8 ounces) whole kernel corn, drained
2 cloves garlic, minced
1 1/2 teaspoons salt
1/4 teaspoon freshly ground pepper
2 to 3 tablespoons chopped hot peppers (fresh or canned) or 1/2 to 1 teaspoon crushed red pepper

3/4 cup Sun-Maid® Seedless Raisins
3/4 teaspoon oregano
1/4 cup cider vinegar
1 can (16 ounces) refried beans
12 flour tortillas
2 cups shredded Cheddar cheese
2 cups dairy sour cream
1/4 cup sliced pimiento-stuffed green olives

Sauté the green peppers and onion in 1/4 cup of the oil until soft but not browned. Add the beef and cook, stirring occasionally, until lightly browned. Skim off excess fat. Add the corn, garlic, salt, pepper, hot peppers, raisins, oregano, vinegar, and 3/4 cup water. Heat gently to boil. Reduce heat, cover, and simmer for 20 minutes. Uncover and cook over medium-high heat, stirring frequently, until the meat mixture is fairly dry, but not burned. Remove from the heat and set aside.

In a large skillet, heat the remaining 1/4 cup oil. Carefully add the refried beans and cook, stirring occasionally, until oil is absorbed and beans are a little crusty. Preheat the oven to 350°F. Grease a 13×9×2-inch baking dish. Spread some of the bean mixture on a tortilla. Spoon about 1/3 cup of the meat down the center of the tortilla, then sprinkle with a little cheese. Fold opposite sides of tortilla over the filling and place the burrito in the prepared dish. Repeat until all the tortillas are filled. Stir the sour cream until smooth and spoon over burritos. Sprinkle with any remaining Cheddar cheese (or grate a little extra) and bake for 20 minutes. Top with the sliced olives.

Opposite: Mexican Meat Ball Soup (page 34), Burritos

Mexican Meat Ball Soup   6 servings

This sophisticated soup combines many flavors and textures. It gives a hint of the variety and subtlety of Mexican cuisine.

1 pound lean ground beef
1/2 cup Sun-Maid® Seedless
   Raisins
1/4 cup long-grained rice
1 teaspoon salt
1/4 teaspoon freshly ground
   pepper
1 1/2 teaspoons dried mint
   leaves, crumbled
1/2 teaspoon oregano
1/4 teaspoon cumin
3 cans (10 1/2 ounces) beef
   broth

1 can (16 ounces) stewed
   tomatoes
1 small head cabbage
   (1 1/2 pounds)
2 medium carrots, cut
   in 1/4-inch slices
2 medium zucchini
   (8 ounces), cut in
   1/4-inch slices
1/4 cup dry sherry

Combine ground beef, raisins, rice, 1/4 cup water, salt, pepper, mint, oregano, and cumin. Mix well. Form eighteen 1 3/4-inch meat balls. Bring beef broth and 1 quart of water to a boil in a large pot. Add meat balls; reduce heat to low and cook for 20 minutes. With a slotted spoon, remove meat balls and set aside. Add tomatoes to the broth. Cut cabbage into 6 wedges. Add cabbage and carrots to boiling broth. Reduce heat and simmer, partially covered, for 8 minutes. Add meat balls and zucchini. Simmer 2 minutes longer. Lace with sherry and serve.

Arab Pocket-Bread Supper   4 servings

Pita bread filled with meat balls, raisins, salad, and a hearty yogurt dressing makes a one-dish meal that is also portable.

1 pound ground lamb or
   lean ground beef
3/4 cup fresh bread crumbs
1/2 cup Sun-Maid® Seedless
   Raisins
1 egg
1/4 cup chopped parsley
1 teaspoon minced garlic
3/4 teaspoon salt

4 pita breads
2 cups torn salad
   greens, lightly packed
1/2 cup grated carrot
1/2 cup thinly sliced
   scallions
1 large tomato, diced
   Middle East Dressing
   (page 35)

Preheat the oven to 400° F. Combine the lamb, bread crumbs, raisins, egg, parsley, garlic, salt, and 1/2 cup water in a bowl and mix well. Shape into 16 meat balls and bake, uncovered, in a shallow pan for 20 minutes. A few minutes before they are finished, heat the pita bread. Meanwhile, combine the salad greens, carrot, scallions, and tomato in a bowl.

Break the pita bread in half crosswise and open pockets with fingers. Place 2 meat balls in each pocket. Drizzle with 1 tablespoon Middle East Dressing, top with salad green mixture, and drizzle with a second tablespoon of dressing.

This is a great dish for a teen-age party. Put out the makings and let the guests assemble the sandwiches. A good supply of juice drinks and a favored layer cake are the only extras you'll need.

Middle East Dressing   about 1 cup

1 can (8 3/4 ounces) garbanzo
    beans, drained
1/2 cup plain yogurt
1 tablespoon chopped parsley

1 tablespoon lemon juice
1 clove garlic, crushed
1/4 teaspoon dillweed
1/4 teaspoon salt

Combine all ingredients in a blender container or food processor. Cover and process until smooth. Or mash beans with a fork, add remaining ingredients, and mix well.

Picadillo   6 servings

Picadillo is a Latin American casserole. It's also a good way to extend a pound of ground beef, to stuff green peppers or tomatoes, and to fill empanadas (savory pastry turnovers).

1 large onion, chopped
1 large clove garlic, minced
2 tablespoons vegetable oil
1 pound lean ground beef
1 pound spinach, washed and
    torn into pieces
1/4 pound mushrooms, sliced
1 cup Sun-Maid® Seedless
    Raisins
1 can (16 ounces) stewed
    tomatoes

2 tablespoons chili powder
1 teaspoon salt
1/2 teaspoon cumin
2 cups shredded Cheddar
    cheese
4 cups corn chips,
    crushed
Shredded lettuce

In a large skillet, sauté the onion and garlic in oil until soft but not browned. Add the ground beef and sauté until lightly browned; remove from heat and drain. Stir in the spinach, mushrooms, raisins, tomatoes, chili powder, salt, and cumin. Preheat the oven to 375° F. In a 3-quart casserole place a layer of the meat and vegetable mixture, then cheese, then corn chips. Continue layers, ending with corn chips. Bake, uncovered, for 30 minutes, or until heated through. Serve topped with shredded lettuce.

Accompany a picadillo at a buffet with black beans, yellow rice, and broiled bacon-wrapped bananas. Flan would be a fun dessert.

Ropa Vieja   4 servings

*This traditional Cuban dish is delightfully different. It gets its name
from the fact that the cooked meat is shredded into "rags."*

1 large onion, chopped	1/4 to 1/2 teaspoon crushed
1 clove garlic, minced	red pepper
2 tablespoons vegetable oil	2 large tomatoes, chopped
1 pound beef flank steak	1 small green pepper,
1/3 cup Sun-Maid® Seedless	seeded and chopped
Raisins	1/4 teaspoon cinnamon
2 tablespoons cider vinegar	1/8 teaspoon clove
1 teaspoon salt	

In a large skillet, sauté the onion and garlic in oil until soft but not
browned. Add the flank steak, 1 1/2 cups water, and the remaining ingredients. Bring to a boil, reduce heat, cover, and simmer for 1 to 1 1/2
hours, or until the meat is very tender. Place the meat on a cutting
board. Holding one end of the meat firmly with a heavy fork, "comb" it
lengthwise into strings with a table fork. Turn and repeat on other end
of meat. Return shredded meat to skillet and reheat.

Serve this dish over steamed rice and decorate with strips of pimiento.
Accompany it with refried beans and a salad of avocado and watercress. Flambéed bananas end the dinner on a high note.

Sweet and Sour Cabbage Rolls
4 to 5 servings

*The hearty meat-and-rice stuffing and the sauce both include raisins
for flavor, variety, and food value.*

8 to 10 large cabbage	1 teaspoon salt
leaves	1/4 teaspoon freshly ground
1 pound lean ground beef	pepper
1/2 cup Sun-Maid® Seedless	1/4 teaspoon paprika
Raisins, divided	1 can (16 ounces) stewed
1/3 cup long-grained rice	tomatoes
3 tablespoons minced onion	1 can (10 1/2 ounces)
2 tablespoons chopped	condensed beef broth,
parsley	undiluted
1 tablespoon lemon juice	Dairy sour cream
1 1/2 teaspoons basil	

Blanch the cabbage leaves in boiling, salted water for 3 to 5 minutes;
drain and set aside. Combine the meat with 1/4 cup of the raisins and
the rice, onion, parsley, lemon juice, basil, salt, pepper, paprika, and
1/2 cup water. Mix well. Place a portion of the meat mixture in the
center of each cabbage leaf. Fold in sides, and roll from stem end.

Place, seam side down, in a large skillet. Add the remaining 1/4 cup raisins and the tomatoes and beef broth; bring to a boil. Cover, reduce heat, and simmer for 50 minutes.

Serve in bowls, spooning the raisin sauce over the cabbage rolls and topping with dollops of sour cream.

Whole-grained bread, sweet butter, and mugs of cider would complete this meal.

Tamale Casserole   6 to 8 servings

Beans and rice sandwich, a filling of raisins and pork in this hearty Costa Rican-style dish that's full of flavor.

Rice Mixture

3/4 cup long-grained rice
1 can (16 ounces) stewed
   tomatoes
1 medium-size green pepper,
   diced
1/2 teaspoon salt

1/8 teaspoon freshly ground
   pepper
1 can (16 ounces) garbanzo
   beans, drained
1/2 cup Sun-Maid®
   Seedless Raisins

Pork Filling

3/4 to 1 pound ground pork or
   1 cup ground or finely
   chopped cooked pork
1 medium-size onion, chopped
1 clove garlic, minced
1 can (8 ounces)
   cream-style corn
1/4 cup Sun-Maid® Seedless
   Raisins

3/4 teaspoon salt
1/4 teaspoon freshly ground
   pepper
1/4 cup sliced pimientos
   or 1 can (2 ounces)
   sliced or diced
   pimientos

Combine all the ingredients for the rice mixture in a large saucepan. Add 1 cup water and bring to a boil. Reduce heat, cover, and simmer for 15 to 20 minutes, or until the rice is tender.

Sauté the pork, onion, and garlic in a large skillet until lightly browned, stirring frequently. Stir in the corn, raisins, salt, and pepper and 3/4 cup water and bring to a boil. Reduce heat, cover, and simmer for 10 minutes.

Preheat oven to 350°F. Layer half the rice mixture in a greased 2-quart casserole. Cover with the pork and top with the remaining rice. Sprinkle with the pimiento, cover, and bake for 25 to 30 minutes, or until bubbly.

Sweet 'n Spicy Pork Chops   4 servings

Browned and simmered in orange juice with raisins, tender pork chops are the nucleus of a delicious family dinner.

4 pork shoulder chops,
1-inch thick
2 medium-size onions, sliced
Salt and freshly ground
pepper to taste
1/2 cup Sun-Maid® Seedless
Golden Raisins

1 cup orange juice
1 tablespoon lemon juice
2 tablespoons firmly packed
light brown sugar
1 teaspoon ginger
1/2 teaspoon poultry seasoning
1/2 teaspoon marjoram

In a large skillet over low heat, render a small amount of fat cut from one of the chops. Add the chops and brown on both sides; remove from the pan. Add the onions and sauté until soft but not browned. Return the chops to the pan and sprinkle with salt and pepper. Add the remaining ingredients and bring to a boil. Reduce heat, cover, and simmer for 30 minutes, or until the pork is fork-tender.

Baked acorn squash and sautéed pepper strips go well with this dish. Add an apple crisp for a perfect ending.

Kielbasa Skillet Casserole   6 servings

Simply prepared sausages, red cabbage, and apples combine in a dish of outstanding flavor. Serve with plenty of rye bread. German mustard is the perfect complement.

1 1/2 pounds kielbasa (Polish
sausage) or knackwurst
3 tablespoons butter or
margarine
1 large onion, sliced
1/2 cup Sun-Maid® Seedless
Raisins
1/3 cup cider vinegar or
lemon juice
1 tablespoon prepared mustard
(optional)

1 bay leaf, crumbled
1/4 teaspoon cinnamon
1 small red cabbage,
(about 1 1/2 pounds),
coarsely shredded
6 small new potatoes,
scrubbed
2 apples, cored and
sliced

Slash the sausage at 2-inch intervals to prevent the skin from bursting. Heat the butter in a large skillet and brown the sausage lightly; remove from the pan. Add the onion and sauté until soft but not browned. Add the raisins, vinegar, mustard, bay leaf, cinnamon, and 1/2 cup water, stirring until smooth. Mix in the cabbage, top with the sausage and potatoes, and bring to a boil. Reduce heat, cover, and simmer for 15 minutes; add the apple slices, cover, and simmer 15 minutes longer, or until potatoes are fork-tender. Place the sausage on a warmed platter, surrounded with the cabbage, apple slices, and potatoes.

Opposite: Kielbasa Skillet Casserole

Piperade
2 servings

This is the traditional omelet of the Basques, a hardy people living in the mountains between Spain and France.

1 medium-size onion, chopped
1 medium-size green pepper, seeded and chopped
1 clove garlic, minced
2 tablespoons olive oil
1 large tomato, diced
4 eggs, beaten

1/4 cup Sun-Maid® Seedless Raisins
1/2 teaspoon salt
1/8 teaspoon freshly ground pepper
Chopped parsley

Sauté the onion, green pepper, and garlic in oil until the onion is soft but not browned. Add the tomato and simmer, stirring often, for about 10 minutes, or until the mixture is thickened. Combine the eggs with the raisins, salt, and pepper and add to the tomato mixture. Stir lightly, then cook until the eggs are set. Sprinkle with chopped parsley and serve immediately.

Feature this dish at brunch or a light Sunday supper. It becomes more substantial when accompanied by homemade whole-grain bread, marinated white kidney beans, and cheese.

Ham Rigatoni and Raisins
4 servings

If you can't find rigatoni, this nutty ham and raisin sauce can be served over spaghetti or any favorite pasta.

1 package (12 ounces) rigatoni or spaghetti twists, cooked
1/2 pound (1 1/2 cups) cooked ham, slivered
1 teaspoon finely chopped garlic
1/4 cup olive oil
2 tablespoons butter or margarine

1/2 cup Sun-Maid® Seedless Raisins
1/3 cup coarsely chopped walnuts
1/4 cup chopped parsley
2 tablespoons chopped pimiento
Grated Parmesan cheese

Cook pasta according to package directions. Meanwhile, sauté ham and garlic in oil and butter about 3 minutes. Add raisins, walnuts, parsley, and pimiento. Sauté 3 minutes longer. Drain rigatoni, toss ham-raisin sauce with hot pasta. Serve topped with grated Parmesan cheese.

Just add garlic bread, salad, and red wine to the menu and you're ready for a party. Scoops of assorted flavors of Italian ices served in a glass bowl make a sensational dessert.

Opposite: Ham Rigatoni and Raisins, Tuna Antipasto Salad with Blue Cheese Dressing (page 56)

Raisin-Anise Beef Stew   6 servings

Anise, raisins, and beef are teamed for an unusual flavor treat. Serve this dish in crusty rolls for memorable sandwiches.

2 medium-size onions, sliced
2 tablespoons vegetable oil
2 pounds beef for stewing
    cut in 1 1/2-inch chunks
1 cup Sun-Maid® Seedless
    Raisins

1 can (10 1/2 ounces)
    condensed beef broth
1/4 cup cider vinegar
2 teaspoons anise seed
1 1/2 teaspoons salt
1 pound butternut squash

In a dutch oven, lightly brown the onions in the oil. Add the meat, raisins, beef broth, vinegar, anise seed, and salt, and bring to a boil. Reduce heat, cover, and simmer for 1 to 1 1/2 hours, or until the meat is nearly tender. Check the stew during cooking and if the mixture is too dry, add a little hot water.

Meanwhile, peel squash, cut in half, and scoop out the seeds. Cut in chunks and add to the stew during the last 30 minutes of cooking time. Continue cooking until the meat and squash are very tender.

Variation

Raisin-Anise Beef Sandwiches: Omit squash. Spoon meat mixture into warm sesame seed rolls. Add a dollop of sour cream or plain yogurt. 8 to 10 sandwiches.

Burgundy Lamb Stew   6 servings

Lamb chops braised in a rich wine sauce will warm your heart.

3 slices bacon
1/3 cup all-purpose flour
1 1/2 teaspoons salt
1/4 teaspoon freshly ground
    pepper
6 lamb shoulder arm chops
    (about 2 1/2 pounds)
2 medium-size onions, chopped
1/2 pound mushrooms, quartered
1/2 cup Sun-Maid® Seedless
    Raisins

1 1/2 cups chopped peeled
    tomatoes or 1 can
    (8 ounces) tomato sauce
1/2 cup Burgundy or other
    dry red wine
1/4 cup chopped parsley
2 teaspoons grated
    horseradish

Fry the bacon in a large skillet until crisp; drain on paper towels and set aside. Combine the flour with the salt and pepper; dredge the chops and brown well in the bacon drippings. Remove chops from the skillet and add the onions and mushrooms. Cook until the onions are soft but not browned. Add the raisins, tomatoes, wine, parsley, and horseradish and bring to a boil, stirring. Return the chops to the skillet, basting with the sauce. Reduce heat, cover, and simmer for 1 hour, or until the meat is fork-tender and the sauce thickened. Place on a warmed platter, crumbling the bacon over the stew.

Serve this stew with plenty of crusty bread to mop up the good gravy, a tossed green salad, and red wine. Fruit and cheese would provide a refreshing dessert.

Moroccan Lamb Stew   4 to 5 servings

History books tell us that Moorish nomads invented lamb stew because it could be cooked so easily over an open fire.

1 1/2 pounds lean lamb for stewing	1 teaspoon cider vinegar
1 tablespoon all-purpose flour	1/2 cup Sun-Maid® Seedless Raisins
1 1/4 teaspoons salt	4 small tomatoes, quartered
1 teaspoon paprika	
2 tablespoons vegetable oil	2 teaspoons oregano
1 1/2 cups minced onions	1 teaspoon cumin
2 teaspoons minced garlic	1/4 teaspoon turmeric
1/2 cup dry white wine	Chopped parsley

Trim the lamb of excess fat and cut into 1 1/2-inch cubes. Combine the flour, salt, and paprika, and dredge the lamb. Heat the oil in a large heavy skillet and brown the lamb well on all sides over medium heat. Add the onion and garlic and cook 3 minutes longer, stirring occasionally. Add the wine, vinegar, raisins, tomatoes, spices, and 1/4 cup water and bring to a boil, stirring well. Reduce heat, cover, and simmer for 1 to 1 1/2 hours, or until the lamb is tender.

Sprinkle with parsley and serve with baked cornmeal mush (polenta) or couscous (semolina wheat) and a tossed green salad. Baked apples with honey would be a pleasant dessert.

Indonesian Lamb Stew
6 servings

Exotically spiced lamb and beans are combined in a hearty stew that sticks to one's ribs.

2 pounds lamb shoulder neck
     slices
2 tablespoons vegetable oil
2 medium size onions, sliced
1 clove garlic, minced
1 can (16 ounces) stewed
     tomatoes
1 1/2 teaspoons salt
1 teaspoon chili powder
1 teaspoon turmeric
1/2 teaspoon ginger
1/4 teaspoon cinnamon

1/4 teaspoon crushed red
     pepper
1/4 teaspoon freshly ground
     black pepper
2 tablespoons cider vinegar
1 large cooking apple,
     peeled and chopped
1/2 cup Sun-Maid® Seedless
     Raisins
1 can (20 ounces) white
     kidney beans,
     undrained

In a dutch oven, brown the meat on all sides in oil. Remove from the pot and add the onions and garlic. Sauté until the onions are soft but not browned. Return the meat to the pot and add the remaining ingredients except the beans; bring to a boil. Reduce heat, cover, and simmer for 1 1/2 hours, or until the meat is fork-tender. Add the beans and simmer 10 minutes longer.

This is a no-fooling stew and should be served in soup bowls, accompanied with warm, crusty French bread and a bean sprout salad.

Ham and Banana Bake
4 servings

Try this Southern style (below) or make up your own variations.

4 center slices boneless
     smoked ham (about
     1 1/4 pounds)
4 small bananas, sliced
1/2 cup Sun-Maid® Seedless
     Raisins

3 tablespoons lemon juice
1/4 cup firmly packed light
     brown sugar
3/4 cup shredded coconut,
     divided
Salt

Preheat the oven to 375°F. Place the ham slices in a greased 13×9×2-inch baking dish. Combine the bananas with the raisins, lemon juice, brown sugar, and 1/2 cup of the coconut; season to taste with salt. Spoon the mixture onto the ham slices and sprinkle with the remaining 1/4 cup coconut. Bake, uncovered, for 25 minutes, or until fruit mixture heats through and the coconut begins to brown.

Variation

For a Southern-style variation, substitute 1 can (18 ounces) vacuum-packed sweet potatoes for the bananas.

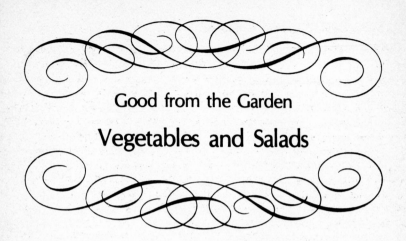

Good from the Garden

Vegetables and Salads

Vegetables and salads take on new dimensions when prepared with Sun-Maid raisins. New flavor combinations and added vitamins and iron make these dishes fine additions to any meal.

Tropical Waldorf Salad   6 servings

Bananas, pineapple, and a coconut dressing perk up an otherwise traditional Waldorf Salad.

Coconut Dressing (below)
2 medium-size red apples, unpeeled
2 cups thinly sliced celery
3/4 cup Sun-Maid® Seedless Raisins
2 bananas, cut into 1/2-inch slices

1 can (8 ounces) pineapple chunks, drained
1/2 cup slivered almonds, toasted
Chilled lettuce cups

Prepare the Coconut Dressing. Quarter, core, and thinly slice the apples and combine with the celery, raisins, bananas, pineapple, and almonds. Fold in the dressing. Spoon the salad into lettuce cups and serve.

Coconut Dressing

Combine 1/2 cup mayonnaise, 1/4 cup shredded coconut, and 1 tablespoon prepared horseradish.

Athenian Stuffed Eggplant   4 servings

Serve this Greek dish as an accompaniment. Add browned ground meat or leftover cooked meat to the filling to make a main dish for 4.

2 eggplants (1 pound each)	1 1/2 teaspoons salt
1 medium-size onion, chopped	1 1/2 teaspoons oregano,
1/4 cup olive oil	crumbled
1/4 pound mushrooms, sliced	3/4 cup macaroni, cooked
2 medium-size tomatoes,	2 cups shredded
chopped	Monterey Jack cheese,
1/2 cup Sun-Maid® Zante	divided
Currants	

Cut the eggplant in half lengthwise and remove the pulp with a paring knife and spoon, leaving a 1/4-inch shell; coarsely chop the pulp. In a large skillet, sauté the onion in oil until soft but not browned; add the chopped eggplant and cook 3 minutes longer. Preheat the oven to 375°F. Stir in the mushrooms, tomatoes, currants, salt, and oregano. Cover and simmer for 5 minutes; remove from heat and stir in the macaroni and 1 cup of the cheese. Spoon into the eggplant shells and sprinkle with the remaining 1 cup cheese. Bake for 20 minutes.

Variation

Brown 1 pound lean ground beef or lamb and add to the filling with the macaroni.

Lentil Raisin Salad   4 to 6 servings

A flavorful and protein-rich salad that is perfect for serving at a picnic.

1 cup lentils	3/4 cup thinly sliced
1 teaspoon tarragon	scallions
1 teaspoon salt	1/2 cup Sun-Maid® Seedless
1/4 cup lemon juice or	Raisins
white wine vinegar	1/4 teaspoon freshly ground
2 tablespoons olive oil	pepper
1 medium-size tomato,	Lettuce leaves
coarsely chopped	Onion rings

Rinse the lentils and place in a large pot with 2 cups water and the tarragon and salt; bring to a boil. Reduce heat, cover, and simmer for 25 to 30 minutes, or until the lentils are tender; drain well. Stir in the lemon juice, oil, tomato, scallions, raisins, and pepper. Mix gently and thoroughly. Cover and refrigerate for about 1 hour, or until the mixture is cool but not chilled. Spoon into a lettuce-lined plate and garnish with a few fresh onion rings.

Opposite: Lentil Raisin Salad, Vinaigrette Medley (page 48), Athenian Stuffed Eggplant

Vinaigrette Medley   4 servings

Blanched zucchini and carrots combine with raw mushrooms in a chilled salad perfect to serve on a summer evening.

3/4 pound small zucchini
2 medium-size carrots
1/4 pound mushrooms,
    quartered
1/3 cup Sun-Maid® Seedless
    Raisins

1/3 cup thinly sliced
    scallions
1 large tomato, cut
    into eighths
Mustard Dressing
    (below)

Cut the zucchini into 1/4-inch slices and the carrots diagonally into 1/8-inch slices; steam or boil for 3 minutes. Drain and combine with the mushrooms, raisins, scallions, and tomato. Pour Mustard Dressing over the vegetable mixture and toss gently. Chill well.

Mustard Dressing   1/2 cup

Dijon-style mustard peps up this traditional oil and vinegar dressing.

1/4 cup vegetable oil
1/4 cup red wine vinegar
1/2 teaspoon marjoram
    or oregano

1/4 teaspoon salt
1 teaspoon grated onion
1/2 teaspoon Dijon-style
    mustard

Combine all ingredients in a small bowl or jar with a tight lid. Beat with fork or wire whisk, or shake until thoroughly mixed.

Greek Spring Salad   6 to 8 servings

Try this spinach salad that has an intriguing combination of colors and tastes.

Sesame Seed Dressing
    (page 51)
6 cups (lightly packed)
    fresh spinach
1/2 cup crumbled feta cheese
1/2 cup Sun-Maid® Seedless
    Raisins

1/3 cup pitted medium-
    size ripe olives
1/4 cup thinly sliced
    radishes
1 hard-cooked egg, grated
4 scallions

Prepare Dressing. Rinse the spinach in several changes of cold water. Pat or spin to dry thoroughly. Tear the larger leaves into bite-size pieces, discarding the stems, and place in a salad bowl. Add the feta cheese, raisins, olives, and radishes. Toss well with the dressing and garnish with grated egg and scallions.

Opposite: Greek Spring Salad with Sesame Seed Dressing

Shrimp Salad

4 to 6 servings

Shrimp atop crisp greens, garnished with a chilled Avocado-Raisin Dressing, are a smash hit as either appetizer or main course.

1/4 cup lemon juice
1/4 teaspoon tarragon
1 pound small or medium-size shrimp, thawed if frozen, shelled, and deveined
1/2 cup Sun-Maid® Puffed Seeded Muscat Raisins
1 small head iceberg lettuce, coarsely shredded
1 small bunch watercress

1 small cucumber, sliced very thin
3 tablespoons butter or margarine
1/2 teaspoon salt
Freshly ground pepper to taste
Avocado-Raisin Dressing (below)

Combine lemon juice and tarragon. Add shrimp and raisins and refrigerate, covered, for 2 to 3 hours. When ready to prepare, drain shrimp and raisins and discard marinade. Pat the shrimp dry with paper towels. Toss the lettuce, watercress, and cucumber slices to combine and arrange on salad plates. In a large skillet, sauté the shrimp and raisins in the butter for 3 to 5 minutes or until shrimp are pink and firm. Sprinkle with salt and pepper. Mound the shrimp mixture on the lettuce, and spoon dressing over all. Garnish with watercress.

This salad is an elegant appetizer, or, served with French bread, it makes a delicious main course.

Avocado-Raisin Dressing

About 1 1/2 cups

This textured dressing is delicious served over seafood, crisp greens, or tomatoes.

1 large very ripe avocado
1 tablespoon lemon juice
3/4 teaspoon salt
Dash freshly ground pepper

1/4 cup Sun-Maid® Seedless Raisins
1/4 cup mayonnaise

Peel the avocado; remove the pit and set it aside. Coarsely mash the avocado with a potato masher or fork. Combine with the remaining ingredients and mix well. Place in a serving dish and put the pit in the center of the dressing to keep it from discoloring; remove the pit before serving. This dressing may be stored in the refrigerator for up to 3 days.

Variation

Avocado-Raisin Dip: Grate 1 small onion and add to the Avocado-Raisin Dressing. Serve with cauliflowerets, carrot and celery sticks, blanched green beans, and green pepper strips.

Sesame Seed Dressing
1/2 cup

Perfect for Greek Spring Salad, this Sesame Seed Dressing will also add sparkle to the Shrimp Salad on page 50 or to a mixed green and tomato combination. Try it on zucchini slices or green beans cooked just until tender-crisp.

1/4 cup olive oil
2 tablespoons lemon juice
1 tablespoon sesame seed
1 clove garlic, crushed

1 teaspoon oregano
1/4 teaspoon salt
1/8 teaspoon freshly ground pepper

Combine all ingredients in a small bowl or a jar with a tight lid. Beat briskly with fork or wire whisk, or shake until thoroughly mixed.

Watercress Salad
4 to 6 servings

Watercress has a bite of its own and is delicious in this unusual salad.

1/3 cup olive oil
1/4 cup white wine vinegar
2 scallions, sliced
1/2 teaspoon salt
Dash freshly ground pepper
1 1/2 cups sliced mushrooms
1/3 cup Sun-Maid® Seedless/ Golden Raisins

1 bunch watercress
Bibb or Boston lettuce leaves
3/4 cup finely diced Swiss cheese
1/4 cup chopped walnuts

Combine the oil, vinegar, scallions, salt, and pepper in small bowl. Add the mushrooms and raisins and stir to coat. Cover and refrigerate for 2 to 3 hours. Wash the watercress and lettuce. Pat or spin dry. Crisp in the refrigerator until serving time.

Place the lettuce leaves on individual salad plates. Toss the watercress with the mushroom mixture and spoon onto the lettuce-lined plates. Top with diced cheese and a sprinkling of walnuts.

Javanese Bean Sprout Salad
4 to 6 servings

Soy-marinated bean sprouts topped with crunchy chopped peanuts make a salad reminiscent of Indonesian cuisine.

3 cups (6 ounces) bean sprouts
1/3 cup Sun-Maid® Seedless Raisins
1/4 cup minced green pepper
1/4 cup minced red onion
1 jar (2 ounces) sliced pimiento, drained

1/4 cup cider vinegar
2 tablespoons peanut oil
1 tablespoon soy sauce
1/4 teaspoon salt
1/4 teaspoon sugar
1/2 cup dry-roasted peanuts, coarsely chopped

Combine and toss the bean sprouts with the raisins, green pepper, onion, and pimiento. Mix the vinegar, oil, soy sauce, salt, and sugar and toss with the salad. Chill for 1 hour, tossing twice during that period. Sprinkle with the peanuts and serve.

Rice al Fresco

4 to 6 servings

Add a rice salad to your repertoire. Pungent red onion and sweet raisins star in this herbed version to present at a picnic, carefully chilled.

1 teaspoon salt	1/2 cup minced green pepper
1/4 teaspoon thyme	1/2 cup minced red onion
1/8 teaspoon saffron	1/3 cup Sun-Maid® Seedless
1 bay leaf	Raisins
1/2 cup long-grained rice	1 small tomato,
1/3 cup vegetable oil	coarsely chopped
3 tablespoons red wine	1/4 cup chopped parsley
vinegar	
1/4 teaspoon coarsely	
cracked pepper	

Bring 2 cups water to a boil with the salt, thyme, saffron, and bay leaf. Stir in the rice and return to a boil. Reduce heat, cover, and simmer for 20 minutes.

Meanwhile, combine the oil, vinegar, and cracked pepper to form a dressing. Drain the cooked rice and turn it into a bowl. Add the dressing and toss well with a fork. Allow the rice to stand for 10 minutes, giving it an occasional toss. Add the remaining ingredients and toss with a fork until well blended. Chill well before serving.

Brown Rice Salad

4 to 6 servings

A nut-flavored herbed salad that is wonderful for a summer supper of cold cuts.

2 cups cooked brown rice	1 tablespoon Dijon-style
1/2 cup Sun-Maid® Zante	mustard
Currants	1 small clove garlic,
1/2 cup coarsely chopped	minced
walnuts	1/2 teaspoon thyme
4 scallions, sliced	3/4 teaspoon salt
1/4 cup chopped parsley	1/8 teaspoon freshly ground
1/4 cup olive oil	pepper
3 tablespoons white wine	Lettuce leaves
vinegar or lemon juice	

In a large bowl, toss the rice with the currants, walnuts, scallions, and parsley. Combine the remaining ingredients except lettuce in a small bowl and beat with a fork until well blended; pour over the rice salad, tossing lightly. Cover and refrigerate for several hours; toss occasionally. Serve the salad in a lettuce-lined bowl, sprinkled with chopped parsley.

Tangy Raisin Slaw
6 to 8 servings

Raisins and pineapple add fresh interest to cole slaw.

3 cups finely shredded cabbage
1 cup Sun-Maid® Seedless
  Raisins
1 can (8 ounces) crushed
  pineapple, drained

1 small carrot, shredded
1 small green pepper,
  chopped
Creamy Slaw Dressing
  (below)

Combine the cabbage, raisins, pineapple, carrot, and green pepper in a large bowl. Toss with the dressing until well coated.

Creamy Slaw Dressing
1 cup

A creamy dressing with lots of zip is very good on cole slaw.

3/4 cup mayonnaise
2 tablespoons cider vinegar
1 tablespoon minced onion
2 teaspoons dry mustard

3/4 teaspoon salt
1/8 teaspoon freshly ground
  pepper

Combine all ingredients in a small bowl, stirring until well mixed and smooth.

Lebanese Tossed Salad
4 servings

Fresh mint and dried currants give tossed green salad a new look.

1/3 cup olive oil
2 tablespoons lemon juice
1 clove garlic, minced
1/2 teaspoon salt
  Few drops hot pepper
  sauce
1 pita bread or 4 very thin
  slices French bread
1 small cucumber

2 cups (lightly packed)
  torn lettuce or spinach
1/2 cup sliced scallions
1/2 cup chopped parsley
1/4 cup Sun-Maid® Zante
  Currants
1/4 cup chopped mint
2 medium-size tomatoes,
  diced

In a small bowl, or a jar with a light lid, combine the oil, lemon juice, garlic, salt, and hot pepper sauce. Separate the pita bread into 2 slices or layers. Toast and break into 1-inch pieces for croutons.

Cut the cucumber in half lengthwise and scoop out the seeds with the tip of a spoon. Thinly slice the cucumber and combine with the remaining ingredients, except the tomatoes, in a salad bowl. Toss with the dressing and serve garnished with the croutons and tomatoes.

Tuna Salad with Pepper

4 servings

Well-flavored tuna fish salad is always a luncheon favorite.

1 large green pepper
3 scallions, thinly sliced
2 medium-size tomatoes, peeled and cubed
1/2 cup Sun-Maid® Seedless Raisins
1 can (7 ounces) tuna, drained and coarsely flaked
2 tablespoons sliced pimiento-stuffed green olives

1/4 cup olive oil
2 tablespoons lemon juice
1 clove garlic, minced
1/2 teaspoon salt
1/4 teaspoon freshly ground pepper
3 drops hot pepper sauce
Cheese sticks or sliced pimientos

Char the green pepper either in the broiler as close to the heat as possible, or on a fork held over the flame on the top of the range; turn frequently. Place in a paper bag. Steam from the hot pepper will make peeling easier. Let stand for 10 minutes. Hold the pepper under running water and rub the skin from it. Cut into 1-inch squares, discarding the seeds and stem.

Combine the green pepper, scallions, tomatoes, and raisins in a salad bowl, tossing to mix. Mound the tuna in the center of the bowl and sprinkle with olives. Combine the remaining ingredients, except the cheese sticks, to form a dressing and pour over the salad. Garnish with cheese sticks and serve immediately.

Variation

Substitute 1 1/2 cups diced cooked chicken for the tuna.

Raisin Tabouli

4 servings

Tabouli, a popular Middle Eastern salad, is a "natural" that stars a minted cracked wheat with California's finest raisins.

1/2 cup Sun-Maid® Seedless Raisins
1/2 cup bulgur
1/2 cup olive oil
1/3 cup lemon juice
1 tablespoon chopped fresh mint or 1 teaspoon dried mint
1/4 teaspoon dillweed
1 teaspoon salt

1/2 teaspoon freshly ground pepper
1 1/2 cups sliced mushrooms
1 cup finely chopped parsley
1 cup thinly sliced scallions
Lettuce leaves
Tomato wedges

Combine the raisins with the bulgur and add 2/3 cup boiling water. Let stand for 30 minutes, then drain off any excess water. Combine the oil with the lemon juice, mint, dillweed, salt, and pepper and toss with the bulgur. Toss in the mushrooms, parsley, and scallions. Cover and chill, tossing occasionally. Serve in a lettuce-lined bowl with tomato wedges.

This is a sensational salad for a buffet. Serve it with a lamb shish kebab and warmed pita bread. Icy-cold watermelon is your answer for dessert.

Raisin-Orange Dressing   1 1/2 cups

This is a good dressing for any fruit salad.

1 cup mayonnaise
1/3 cup Sun-Maid® Seedless
    Raisins

1/4 cup frozen orange juice
    concentrate, thawed

Combine all ingredients and chill.

Picnic Salad Sandwich   12 sandwiches

This is a fun salad — fun to make and fun to eat. Wrap each pita sandwich individually and tote this no-fuss finger food along on your next picnic.

1/3 cup red wine vinegar
1/3 cup olive oil
3/4 teaspoon salt
1/4 teaspoon freshly
    ground pepper
1 scallion, thinly sliced
2 tablespoons chopped parsley
1 package (10 ounces)
    frozen French-cut
    green beans, thawed
    and well drained

1/2 cup Sun-Maid® Seedless
    Raisins
6 pita breads
12 lettuce leaves
2 or 3 medium-size tomatoes,
    peeled and
    cut into chunks
1 jar (6 ounces) marinated
    artichoke hearts
6 hard-cooked eggs,
    chopped

Combine the vinegar, oil, salt, and pepper in a bowl and beat well. Stir in the scallion, parsley, green beans, and raisins; toss to mix. Cover and refrigerate for at least 2 hours.

Gently break the pita breads in half crosswise. With the fingers, force open the "pocket" in each half. Tuck a lettuce leaf into the bottom of each pocket. Top with some of the bean mixture, tomato chunks, artichoke hearts, and chopped egg.

Variation

Picnic Luncheon Salad: Line a platter with lettuce leaves. Cover with the bean mixture and arrange tomato wedges, artichoke hearts, and hard-cooked egg slices attractively on top. Rolled ham slices and cheese sticks make a main dish for 6.

Tuna Antipasto   4 servings

Serve this salad as a first course to dress up a spaghetti supper, or as a cool, light lunch.

1 jar (6 ounces) marinated
    artichoke hearts,
    undrained
1 can (8 ounces) garbanzo
    beans, drained
1/4 cup Sun-Maid® Seedless
    Raisins
1 tablespoon cider vinegar
1/8 teaspoon dillweed
1 can (7 ounces) chunk light
    tuna, drained

1/4 cup thinly sliced
    red onion
    Blue Cheese Dressing
    (below)
4 lettuce cups
4 hard-cooked eggs, halved
    (optional)

Combine and toss the artichoke hearts, garbanzos, raisins, vinegar, and dillweed. Add the tuna and onion, gently tossing. Chill 1 hour. Prepare the dressing and spoon the salad into the lettuce cups. Drizzle with dressing and serve each salad garnished with egg halves.

Blue Cheese Dressing

Combine 1/3 cup dairy sour cream, 2 tablespoons crumbled blue cheese, and 1 teaspoon cider vinegar.

Spicy Vegetable Medley   6 servings

Cumin adds an interesting flavor to this vegetable medley, which is good served with roast chicken or pork. Don't overcook!

1 medium-size onion, sliced
2 tablespoons butter or
    margarine
1/3 cup Sun-Maid® Puffed
    Seeded Muscat Raisins
2 small zucchini, sliced
1 package (10 ounces) frozen
    whole-kernel corn, or
    2 cups fresh corn

2 large tomatoes,
    cut into chunks
3/4 teaspoon cumin
1 teaspoon salt
    Chopped parsley

Sauté the onion in butter in a large saucepan until the onion is soft but not browned. Stir in the raisins, zucchini, corn, tomatoes, cumin, and salt. (If the tomatoes are very firm or underripe, add 2 or 3 tablespoons water to the pan.) Slowly heat to a simmer. Stir gently, then cover and simmer for 6 to 8 minutes, or until vegetables are tender. Stir gently and serve sprinkled with chopped parsley.

Herbed Beans and Zucchini

6 servings

An herb-scented vegetable dish that is particularly good when made with garden-fresh vegetables.

1 pound green beans or
    1 package (10 ounces)
    frozen green beans
3 tablespoons butter or
    margarine
1 small onion, sliced
1 small clove garlic, minced
1/2 cup Sun-Maid® Seedless
    Raisins

1/2 teaspoon oregano
1/4 teaspoon rosemary,
    crumbled
3/4 teaspoon salt
1/2 pound zucchini
    2 tablespoons chopped
    parsley

Wash and trim the beans and cut into 1-inch pieces. Heat the butter in a large saucepan and cook the onion and garlic until the onion is soft but not browned. Add the beans, raisins, oregano, rosemary, salt, and 1/2 cup water and bring to a boil. Cover, reduce heat, and simmer for 15 minutes.

Meanwhile, scrub the zucchini with a soft brush. Cut into 1/4-inch slices. Add to beans, cover, and simmer 5 minutes longer, or until beans are tender. Stir very gently to avoid breaking up the zucchini. Spoon into a serving bowl and sprinkle with parsley.

Stuffed Zucchini Boats

4 to 8 servings

Easy to make, attractive on a buffet table, and exactly right for sparking up a family fish supper, these zucchini boats can also serve as appetizers.

4 medium-size zucchini
    (1 1/2 to 2 pounds)
1/2 cup minced onion
1 large clove garlic, minced
1 1/2 tablespoons vegetable oil
1/3 cup Sun-Maid® Seedless
    Raisins

1 teaspoon basil, crumbled
1 teaspoon salt
2 cups fresh bread crumbs
1/2 cup grated Parmesan
    cheese
Shredded Cheddar cheese

Cut the zucchini in half lengthwise and scoop out the center with the tip of a spoon, leaving a 1/4-inch shell; chop the zucchini pulp. Sauté the onion and garlic in oil until the onion is soft but not browned. Add the chopped zucchini and the raisins, basil, and salt. Simmer, stirring occasionally, for a few minutes, or until the excess moisture evaporates. Preheat the oven to 375°F. Remove the zucchini mixture from heat and stir in the bread crumbs and Parmesan cheese. Spoon into the zucchini shells and place the stuffed boats in a 13×9-inch baking dish. Sprinkle the boats with Cheddar cheese and pour 1/3 cup water into the dish. Cover and bake 20 minutes; uncover and bake 5 minutes longer.

Bird of Paradise Salad   6 to 8 servings

Here's a refreshing and edible showpiece for parties and luncheons that's well worth the trouble. Wait for the raves you'll get.

Raisin-Orange Dressing
   (page 55)
1 large pineapple with
   well-formed crown
1 cup Sun-Maid® Seedless
   Raisins

Assorted fresh fruit
   in season, sliced
   or chunked

Prepare the dressing and chill. Cut the pineapple in half through the crown, damaging the leaves as little as possible. Using a grapefruit knife, cut out the fruit from each shell in as large a single piece as possible. Then cut a slice, 3/4 inch thick, from the large, flat surface of each half. Set the rest of the pineapple aside.

Using a sharp paring knife, cut the silhouette of a bird's head, 4 to 5 inches high, from each slice. Attach each to the base of a shell half with picks or metal skewers. Attach cherry halves and raisins for eyes.

Chunk the remaining pineapple, discarding any hard core, and place in a 2-quart measuring cup. Add the raisins and enough assorted fruit to measure 7 cups. Toss gently to combine and spoon into the pineapple shells. Serve with Raisin-Orange Dressing.

Variation

Bird of Paradise Luncheon Salad: Substitute 1 cup cooked, diced chicken and 1 cup cubed, mild Cheddar or Monterey Jack cheese for 2 cups of the fruit. 4 servings.

Baked Carrot-Raisin Medley   6 servings

A creative and healthful casserole to serve with any meal. This dish is a popular dessert in India. Leave off the butter and parsley and enjoy it cold as an unusual dessert.

3/4 cup Sun-Maid® Seedless
   Raisins
1 large baking apple,
   thinly sliced
3 cups thinly sliced carrots
1 lemon, divided

1/4 cup honey
3/4 teaspoon cinnamon
1/2 teaspoon salt
2 tablespoons butter or
   margarine
Chopped parsley

Preheat the oven to 400°F. Combine the raisins, apple, and carrots in a large bowl. Cut the lemon in half and add the juice from one half along with the honey, cinnamon, and salt to the bowl, mixing well. Turn the mixture into a greased 2-quart heat-proof casserole. Thinly slice the remaining lemon half and arrange the slices on top. Cover and bake for 1 hour, or until the carrots are tender. Serve dotted with butter and sprinkled with parsley.

Gratifying Go-Alongs
Accompaniments and Additions

These exciting touches will make the plainest everyday meal a treat. Need a new sauce or relish? Check our bounty of good things made with Sun-Maid raisins.

Grandma's Raisin Stuffing   stuffs a 6- to 8-pound bird

Even Grandma never had it so good.

1 cup thinly sliced celery	1/4 teaspoon freshly ground
1 medium-size onion, chopped	pepper
1/2 cup butter or margarine	6 cups day-old bread cubes
1 chicken bouillon cube	3/4 cup Sun-Maid® Seedless
1 teaspoon poultry seasoning	Golden Raisins
1/2 teaspoon salt	

Sauté the celery and onion in butter until soft but not browned. Preheat the oven to 350° F. Add 1/2 cup water, the bouillon cube, poultry seasoning, salt and pepper; stir until well blended. Combine the bread cubes and raisins and pour the celery-broth mixture over, tossing to combine. Spoon the stuffing into a lightly buttered 1 1/2-quart casserole. Bake uncovered for 30 minutes, or until the top is lightly browned.

Variations

Stuffed Chicken: Preheat oven to 325° F. Spoon the stuffing into a 6-pound roasting chicken and roast for 2 to 2 1/2 hours, or until the internal temperature reaches 185° F and the leg moves up and down easily.

Stuffed Turkey: Preheat oven to 325° F. Spoon stuffing into a 6- to 8-pound turkey. Roast for 3 to 3 1/2 hours, or until the internal temperature reaches 185° F and the leg moves up and down easily.

Fresno Bean Bake   6 servings

*The San Joaquin Valley in California is home to luscious Sun-Maid®
Raisins, and the folks who live there use a lot of them. This is one of
their favorite recipes.*

3 slices bacon	1 can (8 ounces) stewed
1 medium-size onion, chopped	tomatoes
1 clove garlic, minced	3/4 cup Sun-Maid® Seedless
1 can (1 pound 15 ounces)	Raisins
pork and beans	1/4 teaspoon salt
1 package (10 ounces) frozen	1 teaspoon dry mustard
baby limas, thawed	1 teaspoon cider vinegar

Preheat the oven to 375°F. Fry bacon until crisp; crumble and set aside.
Sauté the onion and garlic in 2 tablespoons bacon fat until soft but not
browned. Combine with the remaining ingredients and mix well.
Spoon the beans into a greased 2-quart casserole, cover, and bake for
40 minutes. Uncover and bake 10 minutes longer.

Raisin Rice Pilaf   6 servings

*Rice cooked in a rich, flavorful broth is a savory complement to any
meal. It is a good base for steamed vegetables — serve with cheese
melted over vegetables.*

1 medium-size onion, chopped	1/2 cup Sun-Maid® Seedless
1/4 cup butter or margarine	Raisins
1/2 cup grated carrot	1/4 teaspoon thyme
1 cup long-grained rice	1/2 teaspoon salt
2 1/2 cups chicken broth	1/2 cup chopped parsley
1 package (10 ounces) frozen	1/2 cup toasted slivered
peas, thawed	almonds

Preheat the oven to 375°F. Sauté the onion in butter until soft but not
browned. Add carrot and rice and sauté. Stir until the rice is opaque
but not browned. Add the chicken broth, peas, raisins, thyme, and salt.
Bring to a boil and pour into a lightly buttered 1 1/2-quart heat-proof
casserole. Cover tightly and bake for 20 to 25 minutes, or until the rice
is tender and the chicken broth absorbed. Add the parsley and toss
lightly until the rice is fluffy and the parsley well combined. Sprinkle
with almonds and serve.

Onion-Raisin Relish   2 1/2 cups

Keep a jar of this wonderful relish in your refrigerator. Its tart-sweet flavor adds another dimension to hamburgers or hot dogs.

1/4 cup mixed pickling spice	2 cups diced red onions
1 bay leaf	1/2 cup Sun-Maid® Seedless
1 cup cider vinegar	Raisins
1/2 teaspoon salt	

Tie the pickling spice and bay leaf in a double thickness of cheesecloth and place in a saucepan with the vinegar and salt. Bring to a boil, reduce heat, cover, and simmer for 5 minutes. Combine the onions and raisins in a heat-proof jar with a tight-fitting lid and pour the vinegar mixture over them. Add the spice bag, cover, and refrigerate for 2 to 3 days. Remove the spice bag before serving.

Raisin Cranberry Relish   1 2/3 cups

Here's an easy variation on the traditional cranberry sauce.

1 large tart cooking apple, coarsely chopped	2 tablespoons chopped dried apricots
1 can (8 ounces) whole cranberry sauce	1 lemon, grated peel and juice
1/2 cup Sun-Maid® Seedless Golden Raisins	1/4 teaspoon salt
	1/4 teaspoon cinnamon

In a saucepan, combine all ingredients. Gradually heat to boiling, stirring often. Simmer for 5 minutes. Cool, cover, and refrigerate. Serve chilled.

Raisin-Apple-Cucumber Relish   about 3 cups

Try this relish on an open-face Danish sandwich of pumpernickel and herbed meat loaf. Tender-sweet currants or raisins provide the flavor balance.

1 medium-size cucumber, thinly sliced	1/4 cup thinly sliced scallions
1 medium-size red apple, thinly sliced	1/2 cup cider vinegar
1/3 cup Sun-Maid® Zante Currants	1/4 cup sugar
	1/2 teaspoon dillweed
	1/2 teaspoon salt

Combine the cucumber, apple, currants, and scallions. In a separate bowl, combine the remaining ingredients with 1/2 cup water, stirring until the sugar is dissolved. Pour over the fruit and vegetable mixture, tossing well. Cover and chill, stirring occasionally.

Spiced Pears with Raisins   8 servings

Poached pears are delicious in spiced wine sauce that's chunky with fruit.

1 cup Sun-Maid® Seedless
   Raisins
1 can (8 ounces) crushed
   pineapple
1 cup sugar
1 cup rosé wine
1/2 cup wine vinegar

1 lemon, thinly sliced
6 whole cloves
2 sticks cinnamon
1 bay leaf
8 pears with stems
1 tablespoon cornstarch

In a large saucepan, combine the raisins, undrained pineapple, sugar, rosé, vinegar, lemon slices, cloves, cinnamon sticks, and bay leaf. Bring to a boil, stirring until the sugar is dissolved. Reduce heat and simmer, uncovered, for 15 minutes.

Meanwhile, peel the pears, leaving the stems intact. Place in the wine syrup, cover, and simmer over low heat for 20 minutes. Carefully turn the pears and simmer, covered, 15 minutes longer, or until tender. Remove the pears to a serving bowl. Blend the cornstarch with 1 tablespoon water and add to the wine sauce. Bring to a boil, stirring, and boil 1 minute. Cool slightly before spooning over the pears. Serve chilled, or at room temperature.

Quick Peach-Raisin Chutney   2 cups

An all-around relish that will add zest to your favorite 'burgers, chicken, meat loaf, or pork chops.

1 can (16 ounces) sliced
   peaches, drained
1/4 cup Sun-Maid® Seedless
   Golden Raisins
1/4 cup diced dried apricots
1/4 cup firmly packed light
   brown sugar
1 can (8 ounces) crushed
   pineapple

1 small onion, chopped
1/4 cup cider vinegar
1/2 teaspoon salt
1/2 teaspoon ginger
1/4 teaspoon cardamom or
   cinnamon
1/8 teaspoon crushed red
   pepper
1/4 cup slivered almonds

Place the peaches in a large saucepan with the raisins, apricots, sugar, pineapple, onion, vinegar, salt, ginger, cardamom, and red pepper. Heat to boiling. Reduce heat and simmer, uncovered, for 15 to 20 minutes, or until somewhat thickened. Fold in the almonds and serve warm or chilled.

*Opposite: Quick Peach-Raisin Chutney, Spiced Pears with Raisins,
Cumin-Onion Relish (page 64), Dried-Fruit Chutney (page 64)*

Cumin-Onion Relish   1 cup

This is the best hamburger or hot dog relish we know. Keep a jar in your refrigerator.

1 large onion, finely chopped
1/4 cup Sun-Maid® Zante
    Currants

1 tablespoon cider vinegar
1/2 teaspoon salt
1/2 teaspoon cumin

Combine all the ingredients and mix well. Serve immediately, or store in the refrigerator for up to 2 weeks.

Variation

To make an instant barbecue sauce combine 1/4 cup Cumin-Onion Relish and 1/4 cup chili sauce in a food processor or blender container. Cover and process until the mixture is finely chopped. Use to brush over meat or poultry on the grill.

Dried-Fruit Chutney   4 8-ounce jars

Make this highly seasoned chutney to serve with ham, chicken, broiled steak, or pork, or to make a vegetable meal sparkle.

3 medium-size tart apples,
    diced
1 cup diced pitted prunes
1 cup diced dried apricots
1 cup cider vinegar
1 1/2 cups firmly packed
    brown sugar
1 teaspoon salt

1/2 teaspoon each cinnamon,
    freshly ground black
    pepper, clove,
    coriander, curry powder
1/8 to 1/4 teaspoon crushed
    red pepper
3 cloves garlic, crushed

Combine all the ingredients with 1/2 cup water in a large saucepan and bring to a boil. Reduce heat and simmer, uncovered, for 20 minutes, or until mixture is thick. Ladle into hot sterilized jars. Seal immediately.

Olive-Mustard Relish   1/2 cup

Delicious spread on rye rounds topped with prosciutto or country ham. A plate of fresh broccoli and cauliflower completes a light meal.

1/4 cup Sun-Maid® Seedless
    Raisins
1/4 cup pimiento-stuffed
    green olives
2 teaspoons finely chopped
    onion

2 teaspoons prepared
    mustard
1/2 teaspoon prepared
    horseradish

Combine the raisins, olives, and onion in a food processor or blender container. Cover and process only enough to finely chop the mixture; do not purée it. Stir in the mustard and horseradish, mixing well.

Raw Mushroom Relish   1 cup

This flavorful mushroom-raisin relish is a zippy accompaniment for any meal. Great with a cheese omelet, or serve it as an appetizer spread on rye bread.

10 medium-size mushrooms, quartered

2 scallions, sliced (including some green)

1/4 cup Sun-Maid® Seedless Golden Raisins

1/2 teaspoon salt

1/2 teaspoon oregano

2 tablespoons white wine vinegar

1/8 teaspoon hot pepper sauce

Place all the ingredients in a food processor (use chopping blade) or blender container and turn on and off quickly to finely chop the ingredients without making a purée. Chill before serving.

Quick Fig-Pear Chutney   3 8-ounce jars

Spicy fruit chutney enhances special meat dishes.

3/4 cup chopped dried figs

1/2 cup cider vinegar

1/2 cup firmly packed light brown sugar

1 lemon, thinly sliced

3/4 teaspoon nutmeg

1/2 teaspoon ginger

1/2 teaspoon mustard seed

1/4 teaspoon salt

1 can (1 pound 13 ounces) pears, drained and diced

Combine all ingredients except the pears in a saucepan and bring to a boil. Reduce heat and simmer, uncovered, for about 30 minutes, or until the mixture is thick and clear. Add the pears and simmer 5 minutes longer. Remove from heat and ladle into hot sterilized jars. Seal immediately.

Hot Fruit Mélange   6 to 8 servings

Beautiful and simple: canned fruit, fresh grapes, and California raisins baked in an East Indian sauce lightly laced with curry.

1 can (16 ounces) peach halves, drained

1 can (16 ounces) pear halves, drained

1 pound seedless grapes, removed from stems

1/2 cup Sun-Maid® Seedless Raisins

6 maraschino cherries

4 slices lemon

1/4 cup firmly packed brown sugar

2 tablespoons butter or margarine

2 tablespoons cider vinegar

1/2 teaspoon curry powder

Arrange the fruit in a 1 1/2-quart shallow baking dish. Preheat the oven to 350°F. In a small saucepan combine the brown sugar, butter, vinegar, and curry with 1/3 cup water. Bring to a boil, stir, and pour over the fruit. Cover and bake for 25 minutes. Serve hot.

Spiced Cabbage Relish   1 cup

A different kind of relish to serve with meat, or as a sandwich topper.

1 cup shredded cabbage	Juice of 1 lime
1/4 cup Sun-Maid® Zante Currants	1/4 teaspoon cinnamon
1/2 teaspoon (or to taste) chopped hot green pepper or 1/8 teaspoon hot pepper sauce	1/4 teaspoon salt

Combine all the ingredients and let stand at room temperature for a few minutes before serving.

Note: It's a good idea to wear rubber gloves when handling hot peppers. Don't touch your face before you wash your hands thoroughly.

Zucchini Relish   1 1/3 cups

A quickly made fresh relish your family will love. Toss it with tuna or chicken chunks for an unusual salad.

1 cup shredded zucchini	2 tablespoons sliced scallions
3 tablespoons chopped Sun-Maid® Seedless Raisins or 3 tablespoons Sun-Maid® Zante Currants	2 tablespoons white wine vinegar
	1/2 teaspoon salt

Combine all the ingredients and toss lightly. Cover and refrigerate until well chilled.

Florentine Noodles   6 servings

A glorious, sauced pasta that can also be made with prosciutto or shredded ham substituted for the bacon.

1 package (12 ounces) spinach noodles	3/4 cup half-and-half, warmed
1/4 cup butter or margarine, melted	1/2 cup grated Romano or Parmesan cheese
2/3 cup Sun-Maid® Zante Currants	4 slices bacon, crisply fried and crumbled

Cook the noodles according to package directions. Drain well and place in a large, warmed serving bowl. Toss well with the melted butter, currants, and half-and-half. Sprinkle with the cheese and continue tossing until the cheese melts and the noodles glisten. Serve garnished with the crumbled bacon. Accompany with additional grated Romano cheese and pass the pepper mill.

Radish Topper

1 1/3 cups

A colorful radish and currant cream to use as a topping for open-face sandwiches.

1 cup chopped radishes
(about 12 radishes)
1/4 cup Sun-Maid® Zante
Currants
1/2 teaspoon salt

1/2 teaspoon sugar
1/4 cup dairy sour cream
2 tablespoons chopped
parsley

Combine all the ingredients and mix well. Chill for 30 minutes before using.

Note: Don't make this recipe too far in advance because the color of the radishes will fade into the sour cream.

Madras Apple Relish

1 1/4 cups

Serve this unusual relish with almost any entrée.

1 large, tart apple,
finely chopped
1/4 cup Sun-Maid® Zante
Currants
2 tablespoons cider vinegar

1 tablespoon honey
1/4 teaspoon ginger
1/4 teaspoon cumin
1/4 teaspoon cinnamon
1/4 teaspoon salt

Combine all the ingredients and mix well. Cover and refrigerate for at least 20 minutes before serving.

Raisin Brown Rice

6 servings

A rice dish the whole family will enjoy. Add Cheddar or mozzarella cheese and chopped peanuts to make a main dish.

2 tablespoons butter or
margarine
1/2 cup chopped onion
1 cup sliced mushrooms
1 cup brown rice
1/2 cup Sun-Maid® Puffed
Seeded Muscat
Raisins

2 1/4 cups chicken or
vegetable broth
or water
1 1/2 teaspoons salt
1/8 teaspoon freshly ground
pepper
1/2 cup chopped parsley

Melt the butter in a medium-size saucepan and sauté the onion and mushrooms until the onion is soft but not browned. Add the remaining ingredients except parsley and bring to a boil; stir well. Reduce heat, cover, and simmer for 45 to 55 minutes, or until the rice is tender. Fold in chopped parsley and serve at once.

Sprinkle with 2 cups shredded cheese and 1/2 cup chopped peanuts, heat just to melt if this is to be a main dish.

Savory Baked Potatoes

6 servings

Baked potatoes, embellished with tasty green beans and currants, become party fare.

6 large baking potatoes
1 cup coarsely chopped
   French-cut green beans
   (frozen and thawed or
   fresh and blanched)
1/4 cup butter or margarine

3/4 cup sliced scallions
1/3 cup Sun-Maid® Zante
   Currants
2/3 cup grated Parmesan
   cheese, divided
1/2 teaspoon salt

Scrub the potatoes well and prick in 2 or 3 places. Bake in a 400°F oven for 1 hour, or until fork tender.

Meanwhile, pat the green beans dry. Melt the butter in a 10-inch skillet; add the beans and scallions and sauté until almost tender. Add the currants and sauté 2 minutes longer. Stir in 1/3 cup of the Parmesan cheese and the salt; toss well.

Cut a cross in the top of each baked potato and squeeze the potato from the narrow ends. Fluff the inside slightly with a fork. Top with a generous spoonful of the bean mixture. Sprinkle with the remaining 1/3 cup of Parmesan cheese.

Parmesan Roll-Ups

8 rolls

Here's an easy way to give a convenience bread a homemade touch.

1/4 cup grated Parmesan cheese
2 tablespoons Sun-Maid® Zante
   Currants or chopped
   Sun-Maid® Seedless Raisins
2 tablespoons chopped parsley
1 scallion, thinly sliced

1 can (8 ounces) refrigerated
   crescent rolls
2 tablespoons butter or
   margarine, melted,
   divided
Coarse salt or sesame seed

Preheat the oven to 375°F. Lightly grease a baking sheet. Combine the cheese, currants, parsley, and scallion. Unroll the crescent rolls and separate into triangles. Lightly brush with some of the butter, then sprinkle with the cheese mixture. Roll up from the wide end and place point down on the prepared sheet. Brush with the remaining butter and sprinkle with salt. Bake for 12 to 15 minutes, or until well browned.

Baked Bounty

Breads to Warm Your Heart

What could be more appealing than bread fresh and hot from the oven, or muffins rich with raisins and currants? Any meal or snack will be better, and better for you, with one of these baked treats.

Spiced Oatmeal Raisin Bread   1 loaf

Cut this compact, dark, yeast bread into thick slices to spread with butter. Or cut less thickly for important sandwiches.

1 package active dry yeast	1 teaspoon cinnamon
2 1/2 cups rolled oats	1/2 teaspoon ginger
3/4 cup Sun-Maid® Puffed Seeded Muscat Raisins	1/2 teaspoon nutmeg
1/4 cup vegetable oil	1/4 teaspoon cloves
1/4 cup firmly packed light or dark brown sugar	1/3 cup sesame seed
2 teaspoons salt	1 3/4 to 2 1/4 cups all-purpose flour

Combine the yeast and 1 1/2 cups lukewarm water and stir until dissolved. Add the oats, raisins, oil, sugar, salt, and spices and let stand for 15 minutes. Stir in the sesame seed and about 1 3/4 cups of the flour, or enough to form a firm dough. Work into a ball and knead for 1 minute on a lightly floured board. Place in a greased bowl and turn once to grease the surface. Cover and let rise in a warm place, free from draft, for about 2 hours. (This is a compact bread and will not double in rising.) Punch down the dough and shape into a ball.

Grease a 1 1/2-quart soufflé or round baking dish. Punch down the dough and shape into a ball. Place in the prepared dish, cover, and let rise. Preheat the oven to 375°F. Bake for 20 minutes; reduce the oven temperature to 325°F and bake 30 minutes longer. Turn out onto a wire rack to cool. While still warm, brush the top of the bread with oil.

Steamed Boston Brown Bread   2 loaves

The traditional Boston Brown Bread is unmatched for its moist texture
and rich flavor. Serve warm with plenty of butter.

1 1/4 cups Sun-Maid® Puffed
    Seeded Muscat Raisins,
    chopped
1 cup whole-wheat flour
1 cup yellow cornmeal

1 cup rye flour
1 1/4 teaspoons baking soda
1 teaspoon salt
2 cups buttermilk
3/4 cup molasses

Combine raisins, whole-wheat flour, cornmeal, rye flour, baking soda,
and salt in large bowl. Toss until raisins are well coated. Add buttermilk
and molasses and stir until batter is smooth. Grease two 1-pound coffee
cans (or one 2-pound coffee can). Divide batter into cans. Cover cans
with a square of greased foil. Mold the foil tightly to the cans and tie
snugly with a piece of string. Place cans on a rack in a large kettle of
simmering water deep enough to come halfway up the sides of the
cans. Cover and simmer 2 hours and 15 minutes or until toothpick inserted in bread comes out nearly clean. Invert cans to cool slightly,
then finish cooling on a rack.

Raisin Oatmeal Muffins   12 muffins

Breakfast muffins you'll love, quick and easy to make, as delicious as
they are nutritious.

1 cup whole-wheat flour
3/4 cup rolled oats
1/2 cup Sun-Maid® Seedless
    Raisins
1/4 cup firmly packed light
    brown sugar
1 tablespoon baking powder

1/2 teaspoon baking soda
3/4 teaspoon salt
1/4 teaspoon nutmeg
1 egg, lightly beaten
1 cup milk
1/4 cup vegetable
    oil

Preheat the oven to 400°F. Grease twelve 2 1/2-inch muffin cups well,
or line with paper baking cups. Mix the flour, oats, raisins, sugar, baking powder, baking soda, salt, and nutmeg in a large bowl. In a separate
bowl, blend the egg, milk, and oil. Add to flour mixture all at once,
stirring just until the dry ingredients are moistened. Spoon into the
prepared muffin cups, filling each about half full. Bake for 20 to 25
minutes, or until the muffins are well browned.

Serve hot with a spinach salad and cheese.

Opposite: Steamed Boston Brown Bread, Sour Cream Streusel Coffee Cake (page 72),
    Mini Hearth Loaves (page 73), Raisin Oatmeal Muffins

Sour Cream Streusel Coffee Cake   1 cake

Delightfully tender with lots of raisin streusel layered throughout an apricot-flecked batter.

Raisin Streusel

2 tablespoons butter or
    margarine, softened
1/3 cup firmly packed light
    brown sugar

1 teaspoon cinnamon
1 cup Sun-Maid® Puffed
    Seeded Muscat
    Raisins

Batter

1 1/2 cups dairy sour cream
1/4 cup butter or margarine,
    melted
3 eggs, beaten
2 teaspoons grated lemon
    peel
1 teaspoon vanilla extract

3 cups all-purpose flour
1 cup sugar
2 teaspoons baking powder
1 teaspoon salt
3/4 teaspoon baking soda
1/4 cup chopped dried
    apricots

To prepare the raisin streusel: mix butter, brown sugar, cinnamon, and raisins together until crumbly. Set aside.

To make the batter: combine the sour cream, butter, eggs, lemon peel, and vanilla. In a separate large bowl, combine the flour, sugar, baking powder, salt, baking soda, and apricots. Gently but thoroughly stir the sour cream mixture into the flour mixture. Preheat the oven to 350°F. Grease a 12-cup bundt pan. Spoon 1/3 of the batter into the prepared pan. Sprinkle with half the raisin streusel. Repeat layers, ending with batter. Bake 55 to 60 minutes, or until a pick inserted in the center comes out clean. Let stand on a wire rack for 10 minutes before removing from the pan to cool completely on the rack. Sprinkle with confectioners sugar before serving.

Raisin-Apple Bran Bread   1 9-inch loaf

This dark, farm-style raisin loaf becomes ambrosial when served with a creamy orange-flavored ricotta spread.

2 eggs, beaten
1/3 cup butter or margarine,
    melted
2/3 cup milk
1 cup wheat bran morsel cereal
1 1/3 cups all-purpose flour
2/3 cup firmly packed light
    brown sugar
1 1/2 teaspoons baking powder

3/4 teaspoon salt
1/2 teaspoon baking soda
1 teaspoon cinnamon
1 cup chopped cooking apple
1 cup Sun-Maid® Seedless
    Raisins
Ricotta-Orange Spread
    (page 73)

Grease a 9×5×3-inch loaf pan. Combine the eggs, butter, milk, and bran in a bowl; let stand for 5 minutes. Preheat the oven to 350°F. Mix the flour with the brown sugar, baking powder, salt, baking soda, and cinnamon in a separate bowl before adding to the bran mixture; stir just until flour is moistened. Fold in the apple and raisins and turn the batter into the prepared pan. Bake for 50 minutes, or until a pick inserted in the center comes out clean. Let stand for 10 minutes on a wire rack before removing from the pan to cool completely on the rack. Serve with Ricotta-Orange Spread, if desired.

Ricotta-Orange Spread

Combine 1 cup ricotta cheese with 1 teaspoon grated orange peel and 1/4 teaspoon salt. Mix well and spread on Raisin-Apple Bran Bread.

Mini Hearth Loaves   3 6-inch loaves or 1 9-inch loaf

Miniature loaves make great gifts and freeze well. If baking for the family, you may want to make one large loaf.

1/3 cup butter or margarine, softened	1 teaspoon baking powder
2/3 cup sugar	1 teaspoon salt
2 teaspoons grated lemon peel	1/2 teaspoon baking soda
1/4 teaspoon cinnamon	1 1/2 cups peeled shredded apple
2 eggs	1 cup chopped Sun-Maid® Seedless Raisins
3 tablespoons milk	1/2 cup chopped walnuts
1 teaspoon lemon juice	Lemon Glaze (below)
2 cups all-purpose flour	

Grease three 6×3×2-inch loaf pans. Cream the butter with the sugar, lemon peel, and cinnamon until fluffy. Beat in the eggs until light and fluffy. Beat in the milk and lemon juice. Preheat the oven to 350°F. Combine the flour with the baking powder, salt, and baking soda and add to the batter, stirring just until the flour is moistened. Fold in the apple, raisins, and nuts and spoon the batter into the prepared pans. Bake for 40 to 45 minutes, or until a pick inserted in the center comes out clean. Let stand on a wire rack for 5 minutes before removing from the pans to cool completely on the rack. Drizzle glaze over the loaves and garnish as desired.

Note: The batter may be baked in a 9×5×3-inch loaf pan; increase the baking time to about 1 hour.

Lemon Glaze

Combine 3/4 cup sifted powdered sugar and 1 tablespoon lemon juice.

Irish Soda Bread
1 loaf

An old-style loaf with raisins and caraway seed. It toasts beautifully.

3 1/2 cups all-purpose flour
1/4 cup sugar
1 teaspoon baking powder
1 teaspoon baking soda
1 teaspoon salt
2 tablespoons caraway seed
1/4 cup butter or margarine

1 cup Sun-Maid® Seedless
    Raisins
1 egg, beaten
1 1/3 cups buttermilk
    Melted butter or
    margarine

Grease an 8-inch layer cake pan. Combine the flour with the sugar, baking powder, baking soda, salt, and caraway seed. Cut in the butter until the mixture resembles fine crumbs. Stir in the raisins. Preheat the oven to 375°F. Combine the egg and buttermilk and stir into the dry ingredients. Turn out onto a board with 2 tablespoons flour and knead lightly. Form the dough into a ball and place in the prepared pan. Brush with melted butter and bake for 30 minutes. Reduce oven temperature to 350°F and bake 20 minutes longer, or until a pick inserted in the center comes out clean. Remove from pan and cool on a wire rack.

Panettone
1 loaf

This Milanese Christmas fruit bread is popular throughout Italy. It can be served at any time of the day, starting with breakfast coffee.

1/3 cup milk
2 packages active dry yeast
3 3/4 to 4 1/4 cups all-purpose
    flour, divided
1/2 cup butter or margarine,
    softened
3/4 cup sugar
4 eggs

1 cup Sun-Maid® Zante
    Currants
1/2 cup finely chopped mixed
    candied fruit
1/2 cup chopped almonds,
    divided

Heat the milk until lukewarm (110° to 115°F) and stir in the yeast until dissolved. Add 1/4 cup of the flour and stir until smooth. Cover and let rise in a warm place, free from draft, until bubbly, about 15 minutes.

In a large electric mixer bowl, cream the butter and sugar until fluffy. Add the eggs and beat until fluffy. Blend in the yeast mixture and 1 cup of the remaining flour; beat for 2 minutes at medium speed. Add 1/2 cup of the remaining flour and beat for 5 minutes at high speed, or until the batter is shiny and "sheets" off a spoon. Stir in the currants, candied fruit, and 1/3 cup chopped almonds and about 2 cups of the remaining flour, or enough to make a firm dough. Turn out on a floured surface and knead until smooth and elastic, about 10 minutes. Place in a greased bowl and turn once to grease the surface. Cover and let rise in a warm place, free from draft, until double in bulk, about 1 1/2 to 2 hours.

Grease a 10-inch tube pan. Sprinkle with additional sugar and remaining almonds. Punch the dough down and roll it out on a lightly floured surface into a 15×10-inch rectangle. Starting with the long side, roll up the dough jelly-roll fashion, pinching the seam to seal. Fit into the prepared pan, seam side down, and pinch the ends to join. Cover and let rise until double in bulk, about 1 hour. Preheat the oven to 350°F. Bake for 45 to 50 minutes, or until the top of the bread is browned and the loaf sounds hollow when tapped with the fingers. (If the bread starts to get too brown during the baking, lightly cover the top with a piece of foil.) Remove from pan and cool on a wire rack.

Focaccia
1 loaf

This Italian bread is baked in a flat pan—untopped for use in sandwiches, topped to serve as a pizza.

2 1/2 to 3 cups all-purpose flour, divided
1 package active dry yeast
1 tablespoon sugar
3/4 teaspoon salt
1 cup milk
4 tablespoons olive oil, divided
1/2 cup Sun-Maid® Zante Currants
Topping (below), optional

Combine 1 cup of the flour with the yeast, sugar, and salt in a large electric mixer bowl. Heat the milk and 3 tablespoons of the oil until very warm (120° to 130°F). Beating at low speed, gradually add the warmed milk and oil to the flour mixture. Increase the speed to medium and beat for 2 minutes. Beat in 1/2 cup of the remaining flour, or enough to make a stiff dough. Increase the speed to high and beat for 5 minutes, or until the batter "sheets" off a spoon. Stir in the currants and about 1 cup of the remaining flour, or enough to make a firm dough. Turn out on a floured surface and knead until the dough is smooth and elastic, about 10 minutes. Place in a greased bowl and turn once to grease the surface. Cover and let rise in a warm place, free from draft, until double in bulk, about 45 minutes.

Prepare one of the toppings. Preheat the oven to 450°F. Grease a 15×10×1-inch jelly-roll pan. Punch the dough down and press into the prepared pan. Brush the surface with the remaining 1 tablespoon oil and sprinkle with the topping. Bake for 12 to 15 minutes, or until golden brown. Cut into squares and serve hot.

Toppings

Olive topping: Combine 1/2 cup sliced, pitted black olives, 1/2 cup chopped parsley, and 1/2 cup grated Parmesan cheese.

Onion topping: Cook 3 onions, sliced, in 1/4 cup olive oil until the onions are soft but not browned. Spread over the dough and sprinkle with 1/2 cup grated Parmesan cheese. The onions may be seasoned lightly with salt.

Poppy Seed Dessert Roll

1 cake

This rich yeast-raised cake is a special holiday treat in central Europe, where it is served as a dessert. It is also a wonderful coffee cake.

Dough

1/3 cup plus 1 tablespoon milk, divided	1/3 cup sugar
1 package active dry yeast	2 eggs
2 1/4 to 2 1/2 cups all-purpose flour, divided	1/4 cup butter or margarine, softened

Filling

3/4 cup poppy seed	1/2 cup ground almonds
1 egg	1/2 teaspoon grated lemon peel
1/4 cup sugar	
1/2 cup milk	2 tablespoons butter or margarine
1/2 cup Sun-Maid® Seedless Golden Raisins	

For dough: Heat 1/3 cup of the milk until lukewarm (110° to 115°F). Pour warmed milk into a large electric mixer bowl. Add yeast and stir until dissolved. Add 1/2 cup of the flour and the sugar. Beat at medium speed for 5 minutes. Beat in the eggs and 3/4 cup of the remaining flour. Beat at high speed for 5 minutes, or until the batter is shiny and sheets off a spoon. Beat in the softened butter until the batter is smooth. Stir in 1 cup of the remaining flour, or enough to make a soft, sticky dough. Turn out on a well-floured surface and knead until silky smooth; the dough should be soft. Place in a greased bowl and turn once to grease the surface. Cover and let rise in a warm place, free from draft, until double in bulk, about 45 minutes.

For filling: Process the poppy seed in a blender container at high speed for 2 to 3 minutes, or until the seed is pulverized. (Or mash in a mortar with a pestle until pulverized.) Beat the egg and sugar until light and fluffy. Add the poppy seed, milk, raisins, almonds, and lemon peel, stirring until well mixed. Turn into a small saucepan, add the butter, and cook, stirring, until the mixture is thick. Cool to room temperature.

To assemble and bake: Grease a 10×6×1 1/2-inch baking dish. Punch the dough down and knead on a lightly floured surface until smooth. Cover with a bowl and let stand for 10 minutes. Preheat the oven to 375°F. Roll out the dough into a 20×10-inch rectangle. Spoon the filling over the dough and spread it evenly to within 1/4 inch of the edges. Starting at both narrow ends of the rectangle, roll the dough up until it meets in the center. Place the loaf seam side down in the prepared dish. Brush with the remaining 1 tablespoon milk and bake (do not set out to rise) for 35 to 40 minutes, or until golden brown. Remove from the dish and cool on a wire rack.

Baked Boston Brown Bread   1 loaf

There's nothing square about this bread except its shape. Serve it with baked beans, for sure.

1 1/2 cups all-purpose flour
1 cup cornmeal
1 1/4 teaspoons salt
1 teaspoon baking powder
1 teaspoon baking soda
3/4 cup Sun-Maid® Seedless
    Raisins

3/4 cup buttermilk
1/2 cup molasses
2 tablespoons vegetable
    oil

Grease an 8×8×2-inch baking pan. Combine the flour, cornmeal, salt, baking powder, baking soda, and raisins in a large bowl. Preheat the oven to 375°F. In a separate bowl, blend the buttermilk, molasses, and oil; add to the flour mixture all at once, stirring until well blended. Pour into the prepared pan. Bake for 25 to 30 minutes, or until a pick inserted in the center comes out clean. Cool for 5 minutes before cutting into rectangles and serving. Have plenty of butter on hand.

Classic Raisin Bread   2 9-inch loaves

Raisin bread has long been a special treat. It tastes even better when you make it yourself.

5 1/2 to 6 cups all-purpose
    flour, divided
2 packages active dry yeast
1/4 cup firmly packed dark
    brown sugar
2 teaspoons salt

1 teaspoon cinnamon
1 3/4 cups milk
1/4 cup butter or margarine
2 eggs
2 cups Sun-Maid® Seedless
    Raisins

Combine 2 cups of the flour with the yeast, sugar, salt, and cinnamon in a large electric mixer bowl. Heat the milk and butter with 1/3 cup water until very warm (120° to 130°F). Beating at low speed, gradually add the warmed milk, butter, and water to the flour mixture. Increase the speed to medium and beat for 2 minutes. Beat in the eggs and 1 cup of the remaining flour, or enough to make a thick batter. Increase the speed to high and beat for 5 minutes. Stir in the raisins and about 2 1/2 cups of the remaining flour, or enough to make a firm dough. Turn out onto a floured surface and knead until the dough is smooth and elastic, about 10 minutes. Place in a greased bowl and turn once to grease the surface. Cover and let rise in a warm place, free from draft, until almost double in bulk, about 2 hours.

Grease two 9×5×3-inch loaf pans. Punch down the dough and divide in half. Shape into loaves and place in the prepared pans. Cover and let rise until almost double in bulk, about 1 hour. Preheat the oven to 375°F. Bake the bread for 40 to 45 minutes, or until loaves sound hollow when tapped. Remove from pans and cool on wire racks.

Apricot Twist   1 coffee cake

This yeast twist rises overnight in your refrigerator! It's made to order for a special brunch. Prepare it in the evening and bake it in the morning.

2 1/2 to 3 cups all-purpose
    flour, divided
3 tablespoons sugar
1 teaspoon salt
1 teaspoon grated orange peel
1 package active dry yeast
3/4 cup milk
8 tablespoons butter or
    margarine, divided

1 egg
1/2 cup chopped dried
    apricots
1/2 cup Sun-Maid® Puffed
    Seeded Muscat Raisins
1/4 cup firmly packed light
    or dark brown sugar
Vegetable oil
Glaze (below)

Mix 1 cup of the flour with the sugar, salt, orange peel, and yeast in a large mixer bowl. Heat the milk with 6 tablespoons of the butter until very warm (120° to 130°F). Beating at low speed, gradually add the warmed milk and butter to the flour mixture. Increase the speed to medium and beat for 2 minutes. Beat in the egg and 1/2 cup of the remaining flour, or enough to make a thick batter. Increase the speed to high and beat for 5 minutes. Stir in the remaining 1 cup of flour, or enough to make a stiff dough. Turn out on a floured surface and knead until the dough is smooth and elastic, about 10 minutes. Cover and let stand for 20 minutes.

Meanwhile, grease a large baking sheet. Combine the apricots, raisins, and brown sugar and melt the remaining 2 tablespoons butter.

Roll the dough out into a 12-inch square and brush with the melted butter. Spread the apricot-raisin mixture over the dough and roll up jelly-roll fashion, pinching the ends to seal. Place seam side down on the prepared sheet. Using scissors, cut from the top at 1-inch intervals about two-thirds of the way down through the dough. Pull cut pieces out to the right and left on alternate sides, twisting slightly to flatten. Brush with oil. Cover the dough lightly with plastic wrap, sealing the edges to prevent the dough from drying out, and refrigerate from 2 to 24 hours.

To bake: Preheat the oven to 375°F. Remove the coffee cake from the refrigerator and carefully take off the plastic wrap. Let stand at room temperature for 10 minutes. Bake for 25 to 30 minutes. Spread with glaze and serve warm.

Glaze

Stir 1/2 cup confectioners sugar and 2 teaspoons orange juice together until smooth.

Opposite: Apricot Twist, Classic Raisin Bread (page 77), Sticky Buns (page 80)

Currant Cheese Bread   1 9-inch loaf

This is a moist loaf with crunchy bits of bulgur and chewy currants added for extra flavor interest and nutrition. Superb toasted, too.

1/4 cup bulgur	1 egg, lightly beaten
2 cups whole-wheat flour	3/4 cup milk
3 tablespoons firmly packed light or dark brown sugar	2 tablespoons vegetable oil
2 1/2 teaspoons baking powder	1/2 cup cream-style cottage cheese
1/2 teaspoon baking soda	
1/2 teaspoon salt	
1/2 cup Sun-Maid® Zante Currants	

Combine the bulgur with 1 cup water and let stand for 15 to 20 minutes; drain well. Grease a 9×5×3-inch loaf pan. Preheat the oven to 350°F. Mix the flour, sugar, baking powder, baking soda, salt, and currants in a large bowl. In a separate bowl, combine the egg, milk, oil, cottage cheese, and drained bulgur; stir until well mixed. Add to the flour mixture all at once, stirring just until the flour is moistened. Turn the batter into the prepared pan. Bake 1 hour 10 minutes, or until a pick inserted in the center comes out clean. Let stand on a wire rack for 10 minutes before turning out of the pan to cool completely on the rack.

Sticky Buns   20 buns

A bun recipe that makes two panfuls. Bake two pans and slip one into the freezer to have on hand for a special Sunday breakfast.

3 to 3 1/2 cups all-purpose flour, divided	1/2 cup dark corn syrup or honey
1 package active dry yeast	1 1/2 cups firmly packed light brown sugar, divided
1/3 cup sugar	1 1/2 teaspoons cinnamon
1 teaspoon salt	1/2 cup chopped nuts
3/4 cup milk	1 cup Sun-Maid® Seedless Raisins
10 tablespoons butter or margarine, divided	
2 eggs	

Combine 1 cup of the flour with the yeast, sugar, and salt in a large electric mixer bowl. Heat the milk with 4 tablespoons of the butter until very warm (120° to 130°F). Beating at low speed, gradually add the warmed milk and butter to the flour mixture. Increase the speed to medium and beat for 2 minutes. Beat in the eggs and 1/2 cup of the remaining flour, or enough to make a thick batter. Increase the speed to high and beat for 5 minutes. Stir in about 1 1/2 cups of the remaining flour, or enough to make a firm dough. Turn out on a floured surface and knead until smooth and elastic, about 10 minutes. Place in a greased bowl and turn once to grease the surface. Cover and let rise in a warm place, free from draft, until double in bulk, about 1 hour.

Combine the corn syrup and 4 tablespoons of the remaining butter in a small saucepan. Stir over low heat until smooth. Divide between two 9-inch layer pans. Using 1/2 cup of the brown sugar, sprinkle half of it into each pan.

Punch the dough down. Divide in half and roll each half into a 10×15-inch rectangle. Melt the remaining 2 tablespoons of butter and brush over the rolled-out dough. Mix the remaining 1 cup of brown sugar with the cinnamon and nuts. Sprinkle half of the mixture over each rectangle and top with the raisins. Roll up jelly-roll fashion from the 10-inch side and cut into 1-inch slices. Arrange in the prepared pans. Cover and let rise until double in bulk. Preheat the oven to 400°F. Bake the buns for 18 to 20 minutes, or until well browned. Invert the buns onto plates and cool slightly before serving.

Pumpernickel Raisin Bread   1 loaf

This dark, raisin-rich loaf is superb served with hearty soups or topped with Swiss cheese for a snack.

2 cups all-purpose flour
2 cups whole-wheat flour
1/2 cup wheat bran morsel
    cereal
1 package active dry yeast
2 teaspoons salt
1 tablespoon freeze-dried
    coffee granules
1/4 cup dark molasses
1 square (1 ounce)
    unsweetened chocolate

2 tablespoons butter or
    margarine
1 teaspoon caraway seed
1 1/4 cups Sun-Maid® Puffed
    Seeded Muscat Raisins
1 egg yolk beaten with
    1 teaspoon water

Combine the flours with the bran and stir to mix well; measure 1 1/2 cups of the mixture into a large electric mixer bowl. Add the yeast and salt. Combine 1 1/2 cups water with the coffee, molasses, chocolate, butter, and caraway seed in a saucepan and heat until very warm (120° to 130°F). Beating at low speed, gradually add the warmed liquid to the flour mixture. Increase the speed to medium and beat for 2 minutes. Beat in 1/2 cup of the remaining flour mixture, or enough to make a thick batter. Increase the speed to high and beat for 5 minutes. Stir in the remaining 2 1/2 cups flour mixture, or enough to make a stiff dough. Turn out on a floured surface and knead until smooth and elastic, about 10 minutes. Place in a greased bowl and turn once to grease the surface. Cover and let rise in a warm place, free from draft, until double in bulk, about 1 1/2 hours.

Grease a large baking sheet. Punch the dough down and roll it out into a 15-inch square. Sprinkle with the raisins and roll up jelly-roll fashion. Place seam side down on the prepared sheet. Cover and let rise until almost double in bulk, about 45 minutes. Preheat the oven to 400°F. Brush the loaf with the egg yolk mixture and bake for 30 minutes, or until the bread sounds hollow when tapped. Cool on a wire rack.

Always-Ready Bran Muffins   24 muffins

*This batter keeps in the refrigerator for up to six weeks. Once baked,
however, these raisin-rich muffins disappear fast.*

3 cups wheat bran morsel
   cereal, divided
1/2 cup shortening
1 cup sugar
2 eggs
2 cups buttermilk

2 1/2 cups all-purpose flour
2 1/2 teaspoons baking soda
1/2 teaspoon salt
1 cup Sun-Maid® Seedless
   Golden Raisins

Grease twenty-four 2 1/2-inch muffin cups. Pour 1 cup boiling water
over 1 cup of the bran; let stand for 20 minutes. Preheat the oven to
400°F. In a large mixing bowl, cream the shortening and sugar until
light and fluffy. Add the eggs and buttermilk and beat well. Beat in the
remaining 2 cups of dry bran. Combine the flour, baking soda, and salt
and add to the buttermilk mixture. Fold in the bran-water mixture and
the raisins. Spoon into the prepared muffin cups, filling two-thirds full.
Bake for 18 to 20 minutes.

Raisin-Coconut Banana Bread   1 8-inch loaf

*A new recipe for banana bread with raisins and coconut to give it that
tropical flavor.*

1 1/2 cups all-purpose flour
1/2 cup sugar
2 teaspoons baking powder
1/2 teaspoon baking soda
1/2 teaspoon salt
1/2 cup Sun-Maid® Seedless
   Golden Raisins

1/2 cup chopped walnuts
1/2 cup shredded coconut
2 eggs, lightly beaten
1 cup mashed, very ripe
   banana (2 medium)
1/4 cup vegetable oil

Grease an 8×4×3-inch loaf pan. Mix the flour with the sugar, baking
powder, baking soda, salt, raisins, walnuts, and coconut in a large bowl.
Preheat the oven to 350°F. Combine the eggs, mashed banana, and oil
and mix until smooth. Add the liquid ingredients to the flour mixture,
stirring just until the flour is moistened. Pour the batter into the
prepared pan. Bake for 50 to 55 minutes or until a pick inserted in the
center comes out clean. Let stand on a wire rack for 10 minutes before
removing from the pan to cool completely on the rack.

Savory Sweets

Desserts to Make Your Mouth Water

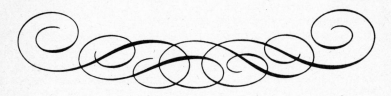

Would you believe that these good things are as wholesome as they are delicious? Try these desserts on the family sweet tooth. Everybody will love them.

California Christmas Cake
2 9-inch loaf cakes

Splurge during the holidays with this magnificent fruit-rich cake. It has the traditional spirited fruitcake flavor.

3 1/2 cups cut-up dried figs
3 1/2 cups sliced dried apricots
3 1/2 cups Sun-Maid® Seedless Golden Raisins
3 1/2 cups coarsely chopped walnuts
1/3 cup brandy
1 cup butter or margarine, softened

1 cup honey
1 tablespoon grated orange peel
6 eggs
2 1/2 cups all-purpose flour
1 teaspoon baking powder
1 teaspoon salt

In a large bowl, combine the fruit and walnuts with the brandy; let stand for several hours until the liquid is absorbed. Grease two 9×5×3-inch loaf pans. Preheat the oven to 275°F. In a very large bowl, cream the butter, honey, and orange peel until fluffy. Beat in the eggs, one at a time, beating well after each addition. (The batter may look slightly curdled.) Combine the flour, baking powder, and salt and add to the butter mixture, beating until smooth. Stir the fruit mixture into the batter. Divide the batter between the 2 prepared pans and spread evenly. Bake for 1 1/2 hours; then increase the oven temperature to 300°F and bake 1 hour longer, or until the cakes are golden and a pick inserted in the center comes out clean. Let stand on wire racks for 20 minutes before turning out of the pans to cool completely on the racks. Store well wrapped in plastic wrap or aluminum foil.

Holiday Fruitcake

1 3¼-pound fruitcake

A fruitcake that's chock-full of fruit and ages like a veteran. Make it well before Christmas.

1 cup Sun-Maid® Puffed
   Seeded Muscat Raisins
1 cup halved candied cherries
1 cup diced candied pineapple
1/2 cup diced citron
1 cup coarsely chopped walnuts
1 teaspoon grated orange peel
1 1/2 cups all-purpose flour

1 teaspoon salt
1/2 teaspoon baking powder
1/4 teaspoon mace or nutmeg
2/3 cup butter or margarine,
   softened
1 cup sugar
3 eggs
2 to 3 tablespoons brandy

Grease a 9×5×3-inch loaf pan well and line with brown paper or foil; grease the paper or foil. Combine the raisins, cherries, pineapple, citron, walnuts, and orange peel; set aside. Mix the flour with the salt, baking powder, and mace. Preheat the oven to 300°F. Cream the butter and sugar until light and fluffy. Add the eggs, one at a time, beating well after each addition. Gradually blend in the flour mixture. Fold the batter into the fruit mixture until the fruit is coated with batter. Spoon into the prepared pan. Bake for 2 hours 15 minutes. Cool completely in the pan on a wire rack. Remove from the pan and sprinkle the cake with brandy. Wrap in cheesecloth and place in an airtight cake tin, or wrap in foil. Let stand for 2 to 4 weeks. Sprinkle again with brandy, if desired.

Harvest Spice Cake

1 cake

A large family-size cake that's simple to make and simply delicious.

1 cup butter or margarine,
   softened
1 1/4 cups sugar
1 tablespoon grated
   orange peel
3 eggs
2 1/2 cups all-purpose flour
1 teaspoon baking powder
1 teaspoon baking soda

1 teaspoon salt
1 teaspoon cinnamon
1/4 teaspoon allspice
1 cup dairy sour cream
1 cup chopped cooking apple
1 cup Sun-Maid® Seedless
   Raisins
1 cup chopped walnuts

Grease a 10-inch tube pan. Cream the butter, sugar, and orange peel until fluffy. Beat in the eggs, one at a time. Preheat the oven to 350°F. Combine the dry ingredients in one bowl and the sour cream and chopped apples in a second one. Add the dry ingredients to the creamed mixture alternately with the sour cream and apple mixture. Stir in the raisins and nuts. Turn the batter into the prepared pan and bake for 55 minutes to 1 hour, or until a pick inserted in the center comes out clean. Let stand for 10 minutes on a wire rack before turning out of the pan to cool on the rack. The cake may be served with whipped cream and a garnish of sliced oranges.

Old World Raisin Torte

1 8-inch torte

A simple dough layered with a raisin-apricot filling to give you a rich, fruity delicacy your family will enjoy. And best of all, it goes a long way.

2 1/4 cups all-purpose flour
1/2 teaspoon baking powder
1/2 teaspoon salt
2/3 cup butter or margarine
2/3 cup sugar
1 tablespoon grated
    lemon peel

1 teaspoon vanilla extract
1 egg
    Raisin Apricot Filling
    (below)
    Confectioners sugar

Combine the flour, baking powder, and salt. Cream butter, sugar, lemon peel, and vanilla until light and fluffy. Beat in the egg. Add flour mixture and stir until well blended. Divide into 3 portions. Chill for 1 hour. Meanwhile, prepare the Raisin Apricot Filling. Preheat oven to 350°F. Pat one portion of the dough into the bottom of a greased 8×8-inch baking pan. Cover with half of the filling. Roll the second portion of dough on a well floured board into an 8-inch square; place on filling. Spread remaining filling over. Roll the third portion of dough into an 8×6-inch rectangle. Cut into strips and place over filling in lattice pattern. Bake for 35 minutes, or until golden brown. Cool completely before cutting. Sift confectioners sugar lightly over torte.

Raisin Apricot Filling

4 cups

A flavorful mixture to slip between the layers of a spice cake, or to roll in a yeast dough for a special treat.

1/2 cup apricot jam
1/4 cup sugar
1 teaspoon cinnamon
1 1/2 cups Sun-Maid® Seedless
        Raisins

1 cup flaked coconut
1 cup chopped walnuts

Combine jam, sugar, and cinnamon. Stir in the raisins, coconut, and walnuts. Mix well.

Apricot-Raisin Dessert Squares   24 squares

Topped with whipped cream or vanilla ice cream, these cookies make a delicious dessert. Served plain, they're a wholesome snack.

1 1/4 cups dried apricots
1 1/3 cups Sun-Maid® Seedless
   Golden Raisins
1/2 cup sugar
2 tablespoons lemon juice
2 tablespoons cornstarch
1/4 teaspoon pumpkin pie spice
3/4 cup butter or margarine,
   softened

1 cup firmly packed light
   brown sugar
1 1/2 cups all-purpose flour
1/2 teaspoon baking powder
1/2 teaspoon salt
1 1/2 cups rolled oats
   Apricot halves
   Mint sprigs

Cut each apricot into quarters and combine in a saucepan with 3/4 cup water. Add the raisins, sugar, lemon juice, cornstarch, and pumpkin pie spice and cook over medium heat, stirring constantly, until the mixture boils and thickens. Cool.

Preheat the oven to 375°F. In a large mixer bowl, cream the butter and brown sugar. Add the dry ingredients in the order given, mixing well. Pat half of the mixture into a greased 13×9×2-inch baking pan. Spread with the cooled fruit mixture. Sprinkle the remaining flour-oat mixture evenly over the fruit and lightly press down with the fingers or the back of the spoon. Bake in the center of the oven for 22 to 25 minutes, until firm in center and topping is crisp. Cool completely before cutting into 2-inch squares. Top servings with an apricot half and a mint sprig.

Figs and Strawberries Supreme   4 servings

A unique combination that makes a quick but regal dessert.

1 pint strawberries
4 dried figs
1/4 cup firmly packed light
   brown sugar

1/2 cup dairy sour cream
2 teaspoons grated
   lemon peel

Just before serving, rinse and hull the strawberries; slice. Stem the figs and thinly slice; combine with the berries. Spoon into a serving dish and sprinkle with the brown sugar. Top with sour cream and sprinkle with lemon peel.

Note: Toss the strawberries with sugar if additional sweetness is desired.

Opposite: Raisin-Pecan Ice Cream Pie (page 96), Figs and Strawberries Supreme, Apricot-Raisin Dessert Squares, Raisin Tartlets (page 119)

Ginger-Stuffed Figs   6 servings

*A dish that's straight out of the **Arabian Nights**—and so simple to prepare.*

1/2 cup finely chopped walnuts
1/3 cup finely chopped
   dried apricots
2 tablespoons finely chopped
   crystallized ginger

1 1/4 cups port, divided
1 package (12 ounces)
   dried figs

Combine the walnuts, apricots, ginger, and 1/4 cup of the port. Cut an opening in the blossom end of each fig and form a cavity with the handle of a small spoon. Stuff with the ginger mixture and pinch closed. Place the figs in a small container with the remaining 1 cup of port. Cover and marinate overnight. Serve with cheese and coffee.

Raisin Carrot Cake   9 servings

A moist, healthful cake that makes a delicious dessert when topped with a rich cream cheese frosting.

1 1/2 cups all-purpose flour
2/3 cup sugar
3/4 teaspoon baking soda
1/2 teaspoon salt
1/2 teaspoon nutmeg
2 eggs
1/3 cup vegetable oil
1 can (8 1/4 ounces) crushed
   pineapple

1/4 teaspoon almond extract
1 1/2 cups finely grated
   carrots
1 cup Sun-Maid® Seedless
   Raisins
1/2 cup flaked coconut
1/2 cup chopped walnuts
Cream Cheese Frosting
   (below)

Grease an 8×8×2-inch baking pan. Combine the dry ingredients. Preheat the oven to 350°F. In a large bowl, beat the eggs with the oil; blend in the undrained pineapple and almond extract. Add the dry ingredients and beat until smooth. Combine the carrots, raisins, coconut, and walnuts and fold into the batter. Turn the batter into the prepared pan and bake for 30 to 35 minutes, or until a pick inserted in the center comes out clean. Let cool completely in pan. Spread with the frosting and serve from pan.

Cream Cheese Frosting   frosting for 1 8-inch cake

A versatile frosting that is particularly good on spice cakes.

1 package (3 ounces)
   cream cheese,
   at room temperature

1/8 teaspoon almond extract
1 1/2 cups confectioners sugar

Beat the cream cheese in a small mixer bowl until fluffy. Add the almond extract. Gradually beat in the confectioners sugar until frosting is smooth and of spreading consistency.

Little Apple Puffs
6 servings

Flaky puff pastry encloses a warm apple and raisin mixture.

4 large tart cooking apples
(about 1 1/3 pounds)
1/2 cup sugar
1 teaspoon cinnamon
Grated peel of 1 lemon
2/3 cup Sun-Maid® Puffed
Seeded Muscat Raisins

1/4 cup chopped walnuts
1 package (10 ounces)
patty shells, thawed
but chilled
1 egg white
Ice cream or sweetened
whipped cream

Peel and thinly slice the apples into a large bowl. Add the sugar, cinnamon, lemon peel, raisins, and walnuts, tossing until apples are well coated with sugar and nuts. Preheat the oven to 400°F. Lightly grease a baking sheet. On a lightly floured surface, roll each patty shell into an 8-inch circle. Spoon about one-sixth of the apple mixture onto the center of each circle. Brush the edge of each circle with egg white and gather the circle into a "bag" around the apples. Seal the pastry and prick with a fork. Place on the prepared sheet and bake for 25 to 30 minutes, or until well browned. Cool slightly.

For a different treat, serve a slice of Cheddar cheese.

Raisin-Banana Foster Flambé
4 servings

A New Orleans specialty that wears well. It's fun to flambé, but use a long match. Serve with demitasse coffee.

4 scoops coffee or vanilla
ice cream
1/4 cup butter or margarine
1/4 cup firmly packed light
brown sugar
1/4 cup Sun-Maid® Seedless
Raisins

1/4 teaspoon cinnamon
2 firm ripe bananas,
sliced
1/3 cup rum
4 maraschino cherries
with stems

Place the ice cream in individual heat-proof dishes or a large heat-proof casserole. Melt the butter and sugar in an 8-inch skillet and add the raisins and cinnamon. Cook over moderate heat 1 minute. Add the bananas and cook 2 minutes, basting with the sauce. Add the rum. When the rum is warmed, remove the skillet from the burner and ignite the rum with a long match. Continue to baste the bananas until the flame dies. Spoon the raisin-banana sauce over the ice cream and serve decorated with cherries.

Note: Ignite rum carefully, out of a draft.

Praline Raisin Cake
1 cake

A crunchy, candy-like frosting tops a luscious raisin-buttermilk spice cake.

2 1/4 cups all-purpose flour
   1 teaspoon baking soda
   1 teaspoon cinnamon
   1 teaspoon nutmeg
   1 teaspoon allspice
   1 teaspoon salt
   1 cup vegetable oil
1 1/2 cups sugar
   3 eggs

1 teaspoon vanilla extract
3/4 cup buttermilk
1 3/4 cups Sun-Maid® Seedless
   Raisins, divided
3/4 cup chopped pecans,
   divided
   Praline Frosting
   (below)

Preheat the oven to 325°F. Grease a 10-inch tube pan or 12-cup Bundt pan. Combine the flour with the soda, cinnamon, nutmeg, allspice, and salt; set aside. Beat the oil, sugar, eggs, and vanilla in a large mixer bowl at high speed for 5 minutes. Reduce the speed to low and add the combined dry ingredients alternately with the buttermilk. Fold in 1 1/2 cups of the raisins and 1/2 cup of the pecans. Pour the batter into the prepared pan and bake for 1 hour, or until pick inserted in the center comes out clean. Let stand on a wire rack for 10 minutes before turning out of the pan to cool completely on the rack. Spread Praline Frosting over the cake and immediately garnish with the remaining 1/4 cup raisins and 1/4 cup pecans.

Praline Frosting
frosting for a 10-inch tube cake

1 cup firmly packed light
   brown sugar
1/2 cup buttermilk

1/3 cup butter or margarine
1 teaspoon baking soda
1 teaspoon maple syrup

Combine the brown sugar with the buttermilk, butter, baking soda, and maple syrup in a saucepan. Cook, stirring occasionally, until mixture reaches the soft-ball stage (234°F on a candy thermometer). Pour into a small mixer bowl. Beat at high speed until creamy. Use immediately. Spread over top of cake, allowing it to drizzle down sides.

Opposite: Raisin-Banana Foster Flambé (page 89),
   Praline Raisin Cake with Praline Frosting

Apricot Mousse   6 to 8 servings

California dried apricots flavor this feathery-light dessert. For an added treat, pass extra Sherried Apricot Sauce at the table.

1 envelope unflavored gelatin	3 egg whites
1 cup Sherried Apricot Sauce	2 tablespoons sugar
(page 121)	3/4 cup heavy cream

Place 1/2 cup cold water in a small saucepan and sprinkle with the gelatin. Cook, stirring constantly, over low heat until the gelatin dissolves. Remove from the heat and stir in the apricot sauce. Pour the mixture into a large bowl, cover, and refrigerate until thickened.

Beat the egg whites in a large mixer bowl until fluffy. Gradually add the sugar, beating until the whites stand in stiff peaks. Set aside. With the same beaters, whip cream until soft peaks form. Spoon 2 tablespoons each of whipped cream and beaten egg whites into the apricot mixture, stirring to mix well and lighten the mixture. Fold the remaining whipped cream and beaten egg whites alternately into the apricot mixture. Spoon into an attractive 6-cup mold or individual dishes. Refrigerate for 6 hours, or until firmly set. Spoon additional Sherried Apricot Sauce over mousse at serving time.

Cheesecake   10 servings

We've taken a hint from European cooks and placed this on a multilayered flaky crust made of Greek phyllo pastry or Hungarian strudel dough.

1/2 cup plus 2 tablespoons sugar, divided	Grated peel of 1 orange
1/4 teaspoon cinnamon	1/2 cup dairy sour cream
1/4 pound phyllo pastry or strudel dough	5 eggs
1/4 cup butter or margarine, melted	1/2 teaspoon salt
4 packages (8 ounces each) cream cheese, at room temperature	3/4 cup Sun-Maid® Seedless Golden Raisins, chopped

Combine the 2 tablespoons of the sugar with the cinnamon. Cut the phyllo dough into 9-inch circles. Place the pastry circles on a damp paper towel and cover lightly with another damp paper towel. Keep the dough covered and moist at all times. Preheat oven to 400°F. Place the circles of phyllo in a 9-inch springform pan, one at a time, brushing each layer with melted butter. Sprinkle every fourth or fifth layer with a little of the cinnamon sugar. Bake for 10 minutes, or until lightly browned, puffed, and crisp. Cool completely in the pan on a wire rack before filling.

In a large mixer bowl, combine remaining 1/2 cup sugar with the cream cheese, orange peel, sour cream, eggs, and salt. Beat at low speed until smooth, then beat at high speed for 4 minutes, or until light and fluffy. Fold in the raisins and pour over the phyllo crust in the springform pan. Bake for 10 minutes; then reduce the oven temperature to 300°F and bake 30 minutes longer. Turn the oven off and let cheesecake stand in the oven 30 minutes longer. Remove from the oven and cool in the pan on a wire rack. Cheesecake will probably crack during cooling.

Variation

Puff Pastry Crust: Substitute 2 frozen patty shells, thawed, for the phyllo pastry. Omit the melted butter. Stack the patty shells and press firmly with heel of hand. Roll out into a 9-inch circle and place in the springform pan. Sprinkle with cinnamon-sugar mixture. Prick the dough well with a fork and chill at least 20 minutes. Bake the crust in preheated 400°F oven for 15 minutes, or until browned. Cool completely in the pan on a wire rack before filling.

Noodle Kugel
6 servings

A kugel, or pudding, is a staple dish in Jewish homes. Unsweetened, it may be served as a main dish or accompaniment; sweetened, as here, it's a lovely dessert.

1 package (8 ounces) wide
   egg noodles
3 eggs
1 cup dairy sour cream
1/2 cup milk
1/3 cup sugar
1/4 cup butter or margarine,
   melted

1/2 teaspoon salt
3/4 cup Sun-Maid® Puffed
   Seeded Muscat Raisins
1/4 cup chopped dried
   apricots

Preheat oven to 350°F. Grease an 8×8×2-inch baking dish. Cook the noodles according to package directions; drain well. Meanwhile, beat the eggs lightly in a large bowl. Add the sour cream, milk, sugar, butter, and salt. Stir until blended and smooth. Add raisins and apricots. Add the noodles and stir until well combined. Turn the contents of the bowl into the prepared dish and bake for 1 hour, or until browned. Cool slightly, then cut into squares. Serve warm or cold.

Variations

Apple-Cinnamon Noodle Kugel: Add 2 apples, peeled and chopped, to the noodle mixture with the raisins, and 1/2 teaspoon cinnamon to the egg mixture. Increase the sugar to 1/2 cup.

Noodle Kugel Accompaniment: Prepare as above, but add 1 cup cottage cheese. Decrease the sour cream to 1/2 cup and the sugar to 1/4 cup.

Elegant Raisin Rice Pudding   8 servings

This is a dressed-up version of an old family favorite, so good you'll want to serve it to company.

6 tablespoons sugar, divided	3 eggs, separated
2 envelopes unflavored gelatin	1 cup heavy cream
1/2 teaspoon nutmeg	Raspberry Sauce (below)
1/2 teaspoon salt	or Rum Raisin Sauce
2 1/2 cups milk, divided	(page 122) or Sherried
1/4 cup long-grained rice	Apricot Sauce
1/2 cup Sun-Maid® Seedless	(page 121)
Golden Raisins	

Mix 4 tablespoons of the sugar with the gelatin, nutmeg, and salt in a large saucepan. Slowly stir in 2 cups of the milk until smooth. Add the rice and raisins and bring to a boil. Reduce heat, cover, and simmer for 20 minutes, or until the rice is tender, stirring occasionally. Beat the egg yolks and the remaining 1/2 cup milk together. Slowly add some of the hot rice mixture to the egg-yolk mixture, beating constantly. Pour back into the saucepan and mix well. Refrigerate until the mixture is cool and will mound when dropped from a spoon, about 1 1/2 hours.

Beat the egg whites until foamy; add the remaining 2 tablespoons sugar and beat until stiff peaks form. Fold into the rice mixture. Beat the heavy cream until soft peaks form; fold into the rice mixture. Spoon the pudding into a 6-cup mold or bowl. Refrigerate for 6 hours, or until firmly set. Loosen the pudding around edge and invert on a dessert platter. Serve with Raspberry Sauce, Rum Raisin Sauce, or Sherried Apricot Sauce.

Raspberry Sauce   1 1/4 cups

1 package (10 ounces) frozen	1 tablespoon cornstarch
raspberries	1/8 teaspoon salt
1/4 cup ruby port	1/8 teaspoon almond extract

Thaw the raspberries. Strain the juice into a small saucepan. Reserve raspberries. Stir in the port, cornstarch, and salt until smooth. Heat to boiling, stirring constantly; boil 1 minute. Cool to room temperature; stir in the almond extract, then fold in the reserved raspberries.

Opposite: Elegant Raisin Rice Pudding with Raspberry Sauce

Sour Cream Pound Cake   1 cake

Pound cake is a reliable standby for any occasion. Try it dressed up with Rum Raisin Sauce (page 122).

1 1/2 cups Sun-Maid® Puffed
    Seeded Muscat Raisins,
    finely chopped
1/4 cup walnuts or pecans,
    finely chopped
2 2/3 cups all-purpose flour,
    divided
1/2 teaspoon salt
1/2 teaspoon baking soda

1 cup butter or margarine,
    softened
2 cups sugar
6 eggs
1 cup dairy sour cream
1 teaspoon vanilla extract
1 teaspoon grated
    lemon peel

Grease and flour a 10-inch tube pan. Combine the raisins and nuts and toss with about 1 tablespoon of the flour. Combine the remaining flour with the salt and baking soda. Preheat the oven to 350°F. Cream the butter and sugar in a large mixer bowl until fluffy. Add the eggs, one at a time, beating well after each addition. Beat for 3 minutes at high speed. Reduce speed to low and add the dry ingredients and the sour cream alternately to the butter mixture. Blend in the vanilla and fold in the raisins, nuts, and lemon peel. Turn the batter into the prepared pan and bake for 1 hour 15 minutes, or until a pick inserted in the center comes out clean. Let stand on a wire rack for 15 minutes before turning out of the pan to cool completely.

Variation

Pound Cake Loaves: Divide the batter between 2 greased and floured 8×4×2 1/2-inch loaf pans. Reduce baking time to 45 to 55 minutes.

Raisin-Pecan Ice Cream Pie   8 servings

This dream pie is quick and easy when you use a ready-made graham cracker crust.

1 cup Sun-Maid® Seedless
    Raisins
1/4 cup sugar
1/2 teaspoon almond extract
1 teaspoon unflavored gelatin
1 can (16 ounces) sliced
    cling peaches, drained

1/2 cup pecan halves
1 quart chocolate mint or
    vanilla ice cream
1 (8-inch) graham cracker
    pie shell

Combine raisins, 1/2 cup water, sugar, and almond extract in saucepan. Bring to a boil, lower heat and simmer 1 minute. Remove from heat. Soften gelatin in 2 tablespoons water. Stir into raisin mixture until dissolved. Cut peach slices in half lengthwise. Fold the peaches and pecans into raisin mixture. Cool. Spoon half of the ice cream into the pie shell. Top with half the raisin-pecan sauce. Spoon remaining ice cream over sauce. Cover with remaining sauce, arranging peach slices in an attractive pattern. Freeze until firm. Let stand at room temperature for 10 minutes before serving.

Creamy Raisin-Apple Tart

8 servings

Here's a rich and attractive free-standing tart that's so easy to assemble you won't believe it.

Crust

1/2 cup butter or margarine, softened

1/4 cup sugar

1 teaspoon grated lemon peel

1/2 teaspoon almond extract

1 cup all-purpose flour

Filling and topping

1 package (8 ounces) cream cheese, at room temperature

1/2 cup sugar, divided

1 egg

1 tablespoon lemon juice

1/2 teaspoon almond extract

3/4 cup Sun-Maid® Seedless Raisins

2 tart cooking apples, peeled and chopped

1/4 cup slivered almonds

1/4 teaspoon cinnamon

1/4 teaspoon ginger

To make crust: Cream the butter with the sugar until smooth. Add the lemon peel, almond extract, and flour and mix well. Pat onto the bottom and 1 inch up the side of a greased 9-inch springform pan. Set aside.

To make filling and topping: Preheat the oven to 375°F. Beat the cream cheese, 1/4 cup of the sugar, and the egg, lemon juice, and almond extract until smooth. Stir in the raisins and spoon the mixture over the crust in the springform pan. Toss the 1/4 cup remaining sugar with the apples and the remaining ingredients. Spread the mixture evenly over the cream cheese filling. Bake for 45 minutes, or until the apples are tender and the filling is set. Cool in the pan on a wire rack. Remove the side from the pan and serve the tart cut into wedges.

Rum Raisin Cake   1 cake

You'd never guess that this rich, flavorful cake starts with a mix.

2/3 cup Sun-Maid® Puffed
　　Seeded Muscat Raisins
1/2 cup chopped walnuts
1 tablespoon all-purpose
　　flour
2 1/2 teaspoons cinnamon, divided
1 package (2-layer size)
　　yellow cake mix
1 package (3 3/4 ounces)
　　vanilla-flavored
　　instant pudding and
　　pie filling

4 eggs
1 cup dairy sour cream
1/2 cup vegetable oil
1/4 cup rum
　　Rummy Glaze (below)

Grease a 12-cup fluted tube pan or 10-inch tube pan. Combine the raisins and walnuts and stir with the flour and 2 teaspoons of the cinnamon until well coated with flour; set aside. Preheat the oven to 325°F. In a large mixer bowl, combine the cake mix, pudding mix, eggs, sour cream, oil, rum, and the remaining 1/2 teaspoon cinnamon with 1/2 cup water. Beat at low speed until combined, then beat at high speed for 5 minutes.

Pour about one-third of the batter into the prepared pan, and sprinkle with about half of the raisin mixture; repeat once, then top with the remaining batter. Bake in the lower third of the oven for 1 hour 5 minutes, or until the top springs back when lightly pressed. Let stand on a wire rack for 15 minutes before removing from the pan to cool completely on the rack. Spoon glaze over the cooled cake, allowing some of it to drizzle down the sides. Garnish with additional raisins and nuts.

Rummy Glaze

In a small bowl, stir 2 cups confectioners sugar and 2 tablespoons rum until smooth. Add 1 tablespoon water a little at a time, until the glaze is of a runny consistency.

Ambrosia   4 servings

From the American South — a luscious dessert that can be served at a moment's notice.

1/2 cup Sun-Maid® Seedless
　　Golden Raisins
1/4 cup Cointreau or other
　　orange-flavored liqueur

1/2 cup shredded coconut
4 oranges

Combine the raisins and Cointreau and let stand for at least 10 minutes. Divide the coconut among 4 dessert plates. Peel oranges with a sharp knife, cutting off all the white pith; cut into sections and arrange on top of the coconut. Spoon raisins and liqueur over orange sections.

Kids in the Kitchen

Good Things Your Children Can Cook

Most young people like to cook. They will especially like using these recipes tailored to their tastes and talents. They'll love the way they taste, and the fact that these dishes will be good for them is a bonus.

Hamburger on a Raft   4 servings

Want to make lunch for your family? Here's a hamburger that makes its own salad.

Avocado-Raisin Dressing
(page 50)
1 1/3 pounds lean ground beef
1/4 cup Sun-Maid® Seedless
Raisins
1 teaspoon salt
1/8 teaspoon freshly ground
pepper

2 tablespoons butter or
margarine, softened
1/8 teaspoon garlic powder
2 hamburger rolls
1/2 head iceberg lettuce

Prepare the Avocado-Raisin Dressing. Cover and refrigerate.

Combine the meat, raisins, salt, and pepper. Shape into 4-inch round patties. Place on rack in broiler pan. Broil about 3 inches from the heat, 5 to 7 minutes on each side, or until done the way you like them.

Mix the butter and garlic powder. Spread on the cut sides of hamburger rolls. Toast during the last 2 minutes of broiling the hamburgers.

Make "rafts" by cutting the lettuce into four 3/4-inch-thick slices. Place each raft on a plate and top with a cooked burger. Spoon a generous portion of the Avocado-Raisin Dressing over each burger. Place half of a toasted roll on each plate. Wow! You did it.

Chili con Corn Bread   4 servings

If you would like to make the dinner tonight, this recipe would be a good choice. Serve it with a salad.

1 pound lean ground beef	1 bay leaf
2 medium-size onions, peeled and chopped	1/2 teaspoon salt
	1 teaspoon chili powder
1 clove garlic, chopped	1/4 cup firmly packed dark brown sugar
1 tablespoon vegetable oil	
1/2 cup Sun-Maid® Seedless Raisins	1 package (8 ounces) corn-muffin mix
1 can (8 ounces) tomato sauce	

Brown the meat, onions, and garlic in a skillet in the oil over medium heat; drain if necessary. Add the raisins, tomato sauce, bay leaf, salt, chili powder, sugar, and 1 cup water. Bring to a boil, stirring constantly. Reduce heat, cover, and simmer for 10 minutes, or until mixture is slightly thickened. Remove the bay leaf.

Preheat the oven to 400°F. Prepare the corn-muffin mix according to package directions. Spoon the meat mixture into a greased 8×8×2-inch baking dish and top with the corn-muffin mix. Spread evenly. Bake for 12 minutes, or until the corn-muffin layer is lightly browned.

Whole-Wheat Bran Muffins   10 muffins

Surprise the family at Sunday breakfast with these delicious muffins.

1/2 cup whole-wheat flour	1/2 teaspoon salt
1 1/2 cups wheat bran morsel cereal	1/2 cup Sun-Maid® Puffed Seeded Muscat Raisins
1/4 cup firmly packed light or dark brown sugar	
	1 egg
1 teaspoon baking powder	2/3 cup buttermilk
1/2 teaspoon baking soda	3 tablespoons vegetable oil

Grease ten 2 1/2-inch muffin cups well, or line with paper baking cups. Preheat the oven to 400°F. In a large mixing bowl, toss the flour, bran cereal, sugar, baking powder, baking soda, salt, and raisins until very well mixed and raisins are coated. Beat the egg lightly in a small mixing bowl and stir in the buttermilk and oil. Add buttermilk mixture to flour mixture all at once. Stir lightly with a fork until the ingredients are fairly well mixed but the batter is still somewhat lumpy.

Spoon the batter into the prepared muffin cups, filling each about two-thirds full. Bake for 18 to 20 minutes, or until muffins are well browned. Remove from pans and serve immediately with butter and jam.

One-Dish Chicken Rice   3 servings

You'll like this delicious casserole because it's so easy to make.

6 chicken drumsticks
   (about 1 1/2 pounds)
1 tablespoon vegetable oil
1 medium-size onion,
   peeled and chopped
1/2 cup long-grained rice
3/4 teaspoon salt

1/2 teaspoon thyme,
   oregano, or basil
1 cup frozen peas
1/3 cup Sun-Maid® Seedless
   Raisins
1 can (8 ounces) stewed
   tomatoes

Preheat the oven to 350°F. In a 2 1/2-quart flameproof casserole, sauté the drumsticks in oil until browned on all sides; add the onion a few minutes before the browning is finished. Add the rice, pouring it in between the drumsticks, and the remaining ingredients. Lightly stir in 1 cup water and bring to a boil. Cover and bake for 25 minutes.

This one-dish supper for a busy day needs only the addition of a salad and fruit-topped ice cream as dessert to complete the menu.

Super Puffed Pancake   4 servings

A super-duper pancake that puffs up to make a crunchy "bowl" that can be filled with surprises. A perfect breakfast for Mother's Day.

1/4 cup butter or margarine
3 eggs
1/2 cup all-purpose flour
1/2 cup milk
1/4 teaspoon salt
4 precooked sausage links

3/4 cup applesauce
1/2 cup Sun-Maid® Seedless
   Golden Raisins
1/2 teaspoon cinnamon or
   nutmeg

Preheat the oven to 450°F. Place the butter in a heat-proof 2-quart casserole and set in the oven to melt the butter and heat the dish. Meanwhile, beat the eggs well in a bowl. Add the flour, milk, and salt. Beat with wire whisk until smooth. Wearing heavy pot mitts, remove the casserole from the oven and tilt so that the butter coats the bottom and sides of the casserole. Pour the remaining butter into the milk mixture and beat lightly until smooth. Pour the batter into the hot casserole and bake at 450°F for 10 minutes; reduce the temperature to 350°F and bake 20 minutes longer.

While the pancake is baking, brown the sausage links well. Drain on paper towels and keep warm. In a small saucepan, combine the applesauce, raisins, and cinnamon and heat over medium heat, stirring until smooth and warmed.

When the pancake is done, remove it from the oven. Spoon warmed applesauce mixture into pancake "bowl" and arrange the sausages around the applesauce. To serve, cut the pancake into quarters with a sharp knife. Lift from casserole with a metal spatula.

G.O.R.P.

G.O.R.P. stands for "good old raisins and peanuts," but you can enliven it with candy-coated chocolate pieces or carob chips.

Combine equal parts of peanuts and raisins. Example: 1 cup peanuts and 1 cup Sun-Maid® Seedless Raisins. Store in a covered jar.

G.O.R.P. and candy-coated chocolate pieces or carob chips are great for a party. Just combine equal parts of peanuts, raisins, and candy-coated chocolate pieces or carob chips. Example: 1/2 cup peanuts, 1/2 cup raisins, and 1/2 cup candy-coated chocolate pieces or carob chips. Serve in small plastic bowls.

Trail Mix Magic   about 4 cups

A quick-energy food that's great to carry on a hike. Add what you want to this recipe. You can do your own thing.

1 1/2 cups Sun-Maid® Seedless Raisins	1/2 cup dried apricots, quartered
3/4 cup sunflower seeds	1/2 cup salted peanuts
3/4 cup banana chips	1/2 cup walnut pieces
	1/4 cup coconut chips

Combine all the ingredients and toss well. Store in a tightly covered container.

Here are some other things you can add: almonds, filberts, pecans; dried figs, apples, peaches, or pears; dates, sesame seed, and candied pineapple; chocolate or carob chips. Who can think of something else?

After-School Snack Balls   24 balls

All but the very youngest members of the family can make this no-cook energy treat.

2 cups Sun-Maid Raisin-Nut Granola (page 105)	1/2 cup toasted wheat germ
	1/4 cup honey
2/3 cup chunky peanut butter	Toasted wheat germ

Combine the granola with the peanut butter, 1/2 cup toasted wheat germ, and honey in a medium-size mixing bowl. Using a fork, stir until the ingredients are well mixed. Shape the granola mixture into 1-inch balls. Roll each ball in wheat germ. (If your fingers get sticky, dip them in the wheat germ, too.)

Opposite: Granola Cookies (page 104), After-School Snack Balls, G.O.R.P., Trail Mix Magic, Raisin Energy Squares (page 104)

Raisin Energy Squares
16 squares

Hiking or biking . . . don't leave home without them. Amaze your friends with your own secret source of energy and bring along some extras to share.

1/2 cup butter or margarine, softened	1/2 cup all-purpose flour
3/4 cup firmly packed light brown sugar	1 1/4 cups Sun-Maid® Seedless Raisins
1 egg	1 cup chopped walnuts
1 teaspoon vanilla extract	1/2 cup carob or semisweet chocolate pieces
1 cup rolled oats	2 tablespoons wheat germ

Preheat the oven to 350°F. Grease an 8×8×2-inch baking pan. In a large mixing bowl, combine the butter, brown sugar, egg, and vanilla. Beat until well blended. Add the oats and flour, stirring until well mixed. Stir in the raisins, nuts, and chocolate pieces. Spread the batter evenly in the prepared pan and sprinkle with wheat germ. Bake for 25 minutes. Cool in the pan on a wire rack before cutting into 2-inch squares.

Granola Cookies
36 cookies

No homemade cookies were ever easier or quicker to make than these. Our homemade granola (page 105) makes them delicious to eat, too.

1/2 cup butter or margarine, softened	1 cup all-purpose flour
2/3 cup firmly packed light brown sugar	1/2 teaspoon baking powder
1 egg	1/2 teaspoon salt
1 teaspoon grated orange peel	2 cups Sun-Maid® Raisin-Nut Granola (page 105)
1/4 teaspoon nutmeg	

Preheat the oven to 350°F. In a large mixer bowl, cream the butter and sugar until light and fluffy. Beat in the egg, orange peel, and nutmeg. Combine the flour with the baking powder and salt and add to the creamed mixture. Beat well. Stir in the granola. Drop rounded teaspoonfuls of the batter onto an ungreased baking sheet. Bake 10 minutes, or until browned.

Tropical Fruit Shake
4 servings

Impress your pals with an out-of-this-world fruit shake.

1/4 cup dried apricots	1 mango, peeled and pitted
1 medium-size, very ripe banana, peeled	2 teaspoons lemon juice
	12 large ice cubes, cracked

Combine the apricots with 1/2 cup warm water and let stand 10 minutes. Place the apricots and their liquid in a blender container. Add the banana, mango, and lemon juice. Cover and process at high speed until smooth.

Remove center of blender cover and gradually add cracked ice, blending at high speed. Blend 1 to 2 minutes longer, or until beverage is very smooth and icy.

Variation

Tropical Fruit Shake Dessert: In a small saucepan sprinkle 1 envelope of gelatin over 1/2 cup cold water; cook over low heat, stirring, until the gelatin dissolves. Add the dried apricots and continue as directed for making fruit shake. Pour into a 5-cup mold, cover, and chill until set. Unmold dessert and top servings with whipped cream.

Sun-Maid Raisin-Nut Granola   about 5 cups

Here's your own recipe for your own granola.

1/3 cup firmly packed light brown sugar	*1 cup Sun-Maid® Seedless Raisins*
1/4 cup vegetable oil	*1/2 cup coarsely chopped walnuts*
1/4 teaspoon salt	
3 1/2 cups rolled oats	*1/2 cup flaked coconut*

Preheat the oven to 250°F. Combine the sugar, oil, and salt with 1/4 cup water in a saucepan and heat, stirring until the sugar is melted. Pour the mixture over the oats, tossing well with a fork. Spread the oats in a 15×10-inch baking pan and bake for 30 minutes, stirring occasionally. Remove from the oven and cool. Add the raisins, nuts, and coconut. Store in a container with a tight lid.

Potato-Apple Skillet   6 servings

Try this combination for a hearty side dish. Enjoy!

2 medium-size onions, peeled and sliced	*1 teaspoon salt*
1/4 cup butter, or margarine, or bacon drippings	*1/4 teaspoon freshly ground pepper*
4 potatoes, peeled and diced	*2 tart cooking apples, peeled, cored, and diced*
1/2 cup Sun-Maid® Seedless Raisins	*2 tablespoons cider vinegar*
3/4 cup apple juice or water	*Chopped parsley*

In large skillet, sauté onions in butter until soft but not browned. Add the potatoes, raisins, apple juice, salt, and pepper and bring to a boil. Reduce heat, cover, and simmer for 10 minutes. Stir in the apples and simmer 10 to 15 minutes longer, or until potatoes are tender. Stir in the vinegar, sprinkle with parsley, and serve.

Variation

Hot Dog Skillet: for a main dish, add 6 frankfurters along with the apples.

Party Tacos
4 servings

A neat Mexican-style dish for a party with a south-of-the-border theme.

1 pound lean ground beef
1 tablespoon vegetable oil
1 medium-size onion,
  peeled and chopped
1 can (15 ounces) chili
  with beans
1/2 cup Sun-Maid® Seedless
  Raisins
1 1/2 teaspoons chili powder
1/2 teaspoon salt

1 bag (7 ounces) tortilla
  chips
2 cups shredded lettuce
1 cup grated Monterey
  Jack or Cheddar cheese
Dairy sour cream
Sliced radishes and
  avocados, tomato slices
  and scallions,
  crumbled bacon bits

Brown the ground beef in a skillet in the oil. Add the onion and cook, stirring, 1 minute. Spoon the excess fat out of the pan. Add the chili with beans and the raisins, chili powder, and salt. Cover and simmer over low heat for 10 minutes.

For each serving, arrange 1 cup chips in the middle of a plate. Surround with 1/2 cup shredded lettuce. Spoon one-fourth of the meat-raisin mixture onto the chips. Top with 1/4 cup grated cheese and a dollop of sour cream. Garnish with one or all of the garnish suggestions.

Pineapple Limeade Punch
10 1-cup servings

Keep a batch of this punch in the refrigerator during hot weather. Serve it to your friends and surprise them with the ice cubes.

1 can (8 ounces) pineapple
  chunks
10 green maraschino cherries
  Mint leaves
1 can (46 ounces)
  unsweetened pineapple
  juice

2 cans (6 ounces each)
  frozen limeade
  concentrate, thawed
4 drops green food
  color (optional)

Drain the pineapple chunks. Add the juice to the punch. Put a cherry or pineapple chunk and a mint leaf in each section of an ice-cube tray. Fill with water and freeze. Combine the pineapple juice and undiluted limeade concentrate. Stir until smooth. Add 2 limeade cans (1 1/2 cups in all) water. Add the food color. Stir and chill well. Serve the punch poured over the fruited ice cubes. Garnish with fresh mint.

Opposite: Pineapple Limeade Punch, Fruited Yogurt Freeze (page 108), Party Tacos

Fruited Yogurt Freeze   6 servings

With a supply of these in the freezer, you can invite the gang over as often as you like.

1/4 cup sugar
1 envelope unflavored gelatin
1 can (12 ounces) peach nectar
1 container (8 ounces)
    peach-flavored yogurt

1 can (8 ounces) crushed
    pineapple
1/2 cup Sun-Maid® Seedless
    Raisins

Mix the sugar and gelatin in a 1-quart saucepan. Stir in the peach nectar and cook over medium heat, stirring constantly, until the sugar and gelatin dissolve. Cool slightly and place the saucepan in the refrigerator until the mixture begins to thicken.

Fold the yogurt and undrained pineapple into the thickened mixture. Place saucepan in the freezer until the mixture is semifirm. Stir in the raisins and spoon the contents of the saucepan into 6 (4- to 5-ounce) plastic or paper drinking cups. Place in the freezer until mixture is very thick, about 30 minutes. Insert a popsicle stick in each cup. Freeze until very firm, 3 to 4 hours.

Gingerbread Men   20 4-inch cookies

Did you know that these cookies are traditional at Christmas? You'll enjoy baking and decorating them.

1/2 cup butter or margarine
1/2 cup firmly packed light or
    dark brown sugar
3 cups all-purpose flour
1 teaspoon salt
1 teaspoon baking soda
1/2 teaspoon cinnamon

1/2 teaspoon ginger
1/8 teaspoon clove
3/4 cup molasses
    Sun-Maid® Zante
    Currants
    Cookie Frosting (page 109)
    Colored sugar

In a large mixing bowl, beat the butter and brown sugar until light and fluffy. Combine the flour, salt, baking soda, cinnamon, ginger, and cloves in a bowl and stir with a fork to mix well.

Add one-third of the flour mixture to the butter mixture. Beat just until combined. Now, add about one-third of the molasses to the batter and beat until well mixed. Repeat the flour and molasses additions two more times. Add 1/4 cup water to the batter and beat a few seconds until the dough is well blended. Cover the dough and chill for about 1 hour.

Preheat the oven to 350°F. Grease 2 large baking sheets. Divide the dough in half and put the part you're not using back in the refrigerator. On a lightly floured surface with a floured rolling pin, roll out the other half of the dough until it is 1/4 inch thick. Cut with a floured gingerbread-man cookie cutter. Use a wide pancake turner to lift the cookies to the cookie sheets. Gently press currant eyes, nose, and shirt buttons into the cookies.

Bake for about 12 minutes, or until the cookies spring back when lightly touched in the center. Do not brown. Let stand 1 minute on the cookie sheet before removing the cookies to wire racks to cool completely. Gather the dough scraps into a ball and refrigerate while rolling out the second half of the dough. Reroll all the trimmings, cut out, and bake. Finish decorating the cooled cookies with Cookie Frosting, additional currants, and colored sugar.

Cookie Frosting

Combine 1 cup confectioners sugar, 1 teaspoon light corn syrup, 2 1/2 teaspoons warm water, and 1/4 teaspoon vanilla extract. Stir until smooth.

Raisin Corn Bread   8 servings

If Mom is serving baked beans tonight, maybe she would like you to make this special corn bread. Maybe she'd like it even if she isn't making beans. Ask her.

1 package (8 ounces)
    corn-muffin mix
1/4 cup butter or margarine,
    melted
1/2 cup Sun-Maid® Seedless
    Raisins

1 can (8 3/4 ounces)
    cream-style corn
1/2 cup grated sharp Cheddar
    cheese, divided

Grease an 8×8×2-inch baking pan. Preheat the oven to 400°F. Prepare the muffin mix according to package directions. Stir in the melted butter, raisins, corn, and 1/4 cup of the grated cheese. Pour the batter into the prepared pan and sprinkle with the remaining 1/4 cup cheese. Bake for 25 minutes. Cut into bars and serve warm with butter and honey.

Pudding Parfaits   6 servings

Would you like to make a dessert for dinner tonight? This pretty, pale green pudding is a good idea.

1 package (3 3/4 ounces)
    pistachio-flavored instant
    pudding and pie filling
2 1/2 cups milk

1/4 cup wheat germ
    Sun-Maid® Seedless
    Raisins

Prepare the pudding according to package directions, but increase the milk to 2 1/2 cups. Spoon half of the pudding into 6 custard cups. Sprinkle each serving with 1 teaspoon wheat germ and some raisins, as many as you think right. Spoon the rest of the pudding into the cups and sprinkle each with 1 teaspoon wheat germ and some more raisins. Chill at least 30 minutes before serving.

Gingerbread   8 servings

This has a lot of ingredients, but is easy to make. It's good warm with ice cream or whipped cream and good cold with applesauce.

1/4 cup butter or margarine, softened	1 teaspoon baking powder
	1/2 teaspoon baking soda
1/4 cup firmly packed light or dark brown sugar	1 1/2 teaspoons ginger
	1 teaspoon cinnamon
1/4 cup honey	1 teaspoon nutmeg
1/4 cup molasses	3/4 teaspoon salt
2 eggs, lightly beaten	Grated peel of 1 orange
3/4 cup orange juice	3/4 cup Sun-Maid® Zante
2 cups all-purpose flour	Currants

Grease an 8×8×2-inch pan. In a large bowl, beat the butter and brown sugar until smooth and thick. Add the honey and molasses and beat again until smooth. Blend in the eggs and then the orange juice. Preheat the oven to 350°F.

Measure the flour, baking powder, baking soda, ginger, cinnamon, nutmeg, and salt in another bowl. Add the orange peel and currants and stir with a fork to mix. Using a spoon, stir the flour mixture into the butter mixture until well mixed. Pour the batter into the prepared pan and bake for 40 minutes, or until a pick inserted in the center comes out clean. Let stand on a wire rack for 15 minutes before cutting and serving.

Apple Spinach Salad   4 servings

Dieting has never been so delicious! This salad plus a little protein is low-calorie dynamite.

1 large red eating apple	3 tablespoons sesame seed
3 tablespoons cider vinegar	1/2 cup Sun-Maid® Seedless Raisins
1/2 teaspoon salt	
Dash freshly ground pepper	4 cups (lightly packed) fresh spinach
4 scallions, thinly sliced	2 hard-cooked eggs, chopped
3 tablespoons butter or margarine	

Peel, quarter, core, and thinly slice the apple. Over a small bowl, cut each slice into thirds. Add the vinegar, salt, pepper, and scallions. Heat the butter in a small heavy skillet until it bubbles. Add the sesame seed and cook, stirring over medium-low heat until the seeds are lightly browned. Stir in the raisins and cook 1 minute longer. Add raisin and butter mixture to the apple mixture. Stir until well combined and set aside.

Rinse the spinach well in cool water and pat or spin dry. Stem the spinach and place the leaves in a large salad bowl. Add the apple mixture to the spinach and toss until well combined. Sprinkle with the chopped eggs and serve with ice-cold skim milk and sticks of Swiss cheese.

Vegetable Medley

6 servings

Vegetable combinations are one of the best and most interesting ways to have a nutritious and well-balanced diet.

3 medium-size carrots, peeled
1/2 medium-size head cauliflower
3 tablespoons butter or margarine
1 medium-size onion, peeled and sliced
1/2 cup Sun-Maid® Seedless Raisins

1/2 teaspoon oregano
1 cube chicken bouillon, crumbled
1/2 teaspoon salt
1/4 teaspoon freshly ground pepper
1 medium-size zucchini, unpeeled

Slice the carrots 1/4 inch thick. Break the cauliflower into flowerets and slice about 1/3 inch thick. Set the carrots and cauliflower aside.

In a large skillet, heat the butter until it bubbles. Add the onion and sauté until it is soft but not browned. Add 1/2 cup water and the raisins, oregano, chicken bouillon, salt, and pepper. Stir until the bouillon dissolves. Add the carrots and cauliflower and bring to a boil. Reduce heat, cover, and simmer for 10 minutes.

Meanwhile, scrub the zucchini and slice 1/4 inch thick. Add to the skillet and simmer 5 minutes longer.

Carrot Raisin Salad

4 servings

Do you enjoy making salads? Here's a pretty one that Mom would probably be happy to have you make.

1 can (8 ounces) crushed pineapple
1 tablespoon cornstarch
1/4 teaspoon dry mustard
1/4 teaspoon salt
2 tablespoons cider vinegar

2 tablespoons mayonnaise
2 cups shredded, peeled carrots
1/2 cup Sun-Maid® Zante Currants
4 lettuce cups

In medium-size saucepan, combine the pineapple, cornstarch, mustard, and salt. Cook over medium heat, stirring constantly, until the mixture boils and thickens. Remove from heat. Stir in the vinegar and refrigerate until well chilled. Gently stir in the mayonnaise. Mix the carrots and currants in a bowl. Add the pineapple mixture and gently stir to combine. Spoon into lettuce cups and serve on individual salad plates.

Lunch Box Highlight

Next time you fix a peanut butter sandwich, skip the jam or jelly and use raisins instead. It tastes great! And when you put raisins in your sandwich, nothing will drip!

"After 3" Nibblers   5 cups

Do you like fixing your own snacks? Here's an easy mix that you'll enjoy preparing and eating.

2 tablespoons butter or margarine   1/2 cup Sun-Maid®
1 1/2 teaspoons soy sauce   Seedless Raisins
1/8 teaspoon garlic powder   1/2 cup pecan halves
2 cups thin pretzel sticks   1/2 cup salted peanuts
1 cup tiny cheese-flavored crackers
1/2 cup Sun-Maid® Seedless
    Golden Raisins

Preheat the oven to 250°F. In a small saucepan, melt the butter. Add the soy sauce and garlic powder and remove from the heat. Combine the remaining ingredients in a 13×9×2-inch pan. Stir the butter mixture and drizzle it over the contents of the pan. Toss the mixture to combine well. Bake for 20 minutes, stirring twice.

Tofu Omelet   2 servings

Ask Mom if you can invite a friend for lunch. Then make this one-dish meal. Tofu is soy bean curd and is used in many oriental recipes. It's high in protein and adds delicious flavor.

1/4 pound tofu (bean curd)   3 eggs
3 tablespoons Sun-Maid® Zante   1/2 teaspoon salt
    Currants   1/8 teaspoon freshly ground
1 tablespoon sliced scallions   pepper
    (optional)   2 tablespoons butter or
1 cup shredded lettuce   margarine
1 can (8 ounces) stewed tomatoes

Cut the bean curd into 1/2-inch cubes. Drain well on paper towels. In a small bowl, combine the bean curd, currants, and scallions. Set aside with the shredded lettuce next to it. Place the stewed tomatoes in a small saucepan. Coarsely chop them with a wooden spoon. Let them heat while you prepare the rest of the lunch.

In a small bowl, beat the eggs, salt, and pepper with 2 tablespoons water until smooth and frothy. Heat the butter in a 10-inch skillet over medium heat. Tilt the pan so that the butter covers the entire bottom. Add the egg mixture. Cook without stirring until partially set, then lift the edge with a metal spatula and tilt the skillet slightly to let some of the uncooked portion run under the omelet. Cook until set. Remove the pan from the heat and spoon the bean curd mixture onto one half of the omelet. Top with the lettuce. Tilt the skillet and fold the other half of the omelet over the filling.

With two pancake turners, lift the omelet onto a platter. Top with the warm stewed tomatoes and serve with crusty slices of French bread.

Practice making omelets. They're just a little tricky.

Banana Bonanza
6 servings

Here's your own recipe for a spectacular-looking banana split. Make it for dessert next time you have friends stay overnight.

2/3 cup shredded coconut
1/2 cup Sun-Maid® Zante
 Currants or chopped
 Sun-Maid® Seedless
 Raisins
1 1/2 pints of your favorite
 ice cream flavor

3 large bananas
1 jar (8 ounces) caramel
 ice-cream sauce
1/3 cup (about) carob chips
 or semisweet chocolate
 pieces

Combine the coconut and currants on waxed paper or a plate. Scoop out the ice cream in 6 nice round balls. Quickly roll in coconut mixture until well coated. (If dessert won't be served immediately, place the coated ice-cream balls on a plate that's been covered with a sheet of waxed paper. Keep in the freezer until ready to use.)

To serve, remove the ice-cream balls from the freezer about 10 minutes before serving. Meanwhile, peel the bananas and split in half lengthwise. Then cut in half crosswise. Divide ice-cream balls among 6 shallow dessert bowls. Slip two banana pieces alongside the ice cream, then pour caramel sauce over. Sprinkle with carob chips and serve immediately. Delish!

Baked Apples
4 servings

For a terrific after-school snack, try these baked apples.

4 large tart baking apples
1/4 cup firmly packed brown
 sugar
1/4 cup Sun-Maid® Seedless
 Raisins
2 tablespoons butter or
 margarine, softened

1/2 teaspoon cinnamon
1/2 cup maple or pancake
 syrup
1/2 cup apple juice

Core the apples with an apple corer. Starting at the stem end, peel off the skin from the top half of the apple. Mix the brown sugar, raisins, butter, and cinnamon. Press the mixture into the empty core in each apple. Place the apples in a small baking dish. Pour the syrup and juice over the apples. Bake the apples in a 350°F oven for 45 minutes, or until the apples feel tender when pierced with a cooking fork. Spoon the juice in the baking dish over the apples 2 or 3 times during baking. Serve warm or chilled.

Snacks and Raisin Specialties
Small Wonders to Brighten Odd Moments

Concentrated food energy, nutrition, and convenience combine to make raisins the perfect quick-energy food. Hikers and climbers for years have used mixtures of raisins and other dried fruit for light, easy-to-carry pick-ups. Now everybody can get in on a good thing: you don't *have* to be athletic to enjoy these treats.

Sugar Plums   30 sugar plums

Festive at holiday-time, these little frosted treats are greatly appreciated all year 'round.

1 cup dried figs,
    stems removed
1/2 cup dried apricots
1/2 cup Sun-Maid® Seedless
    Raisins

1/2 cup walnuts
1 orange, unpeeled,
    quartered
1 1/2 cups (about) shredded
    coconut, toasted

Combine the figs, apricots, raisins, nuts, and orange in a food processor. (Use chopping blade.) Cover and process until the fruit is finely chopped and well mixed. (Or grind fruit in a food grinder fitted with finest blade; mix well.) Shape tablespoonfuls of the mixture into balls. Roll in coconut until coated.

To toast coconut, spread in shallow baking pan. Bake at 300°F for 15 minutes, or until lightly browned, stirring often.

Variations

Stir 1/2 cup peanut butter into the ground fruit mixture; mix well.

Add 1/4 cup toasted sesame seed and 1/4 cup honey to the ground fruit mixture; mix well.

Opposite: Hermits (page 117), Raisin Turnovers (page 116), "After 3" Nibblers (page 112), Raisin-Nut Cups (page 116), Apricot-Pineapple Jam (page 117), Sugar Plums

Raisin Turnovers

20 turnovers

Dainty turnovers filled with Muscat Raisins.

2/3 cup Sun-Maid® Puffed
Seeded Muscat Raisins,
chopped
1/4 cup finely chopped citron
1/2 cup sugar

1 teaspoon cornstarch
1 teaspoon grated lemon
peel
1 tablespoon lemon juice

Dough

1 3/4 cups all-purpose flour
1 teaspoon salt
2/3 cup shortening

6 tablespoons (about) milk,
divided
Sugar

In a small saucepan, combine the raisins and citron with 1/3 cup water and bring to a boil. Reduce heat and simmer, uncovered, for 3 minutes. Mix the sugar and cornstarch and add to the raisin mixture. Cook, stirring constantly, until the mixture boils; lower heat and simmer for 1 minute, stirring constantly. Remove the pan from the heat and stir in the lemon peel and juice. Cool completely.

To prepare the dough: Mix the flour and salt in a bowl and cut in the shortening with a pastry blender until crumbly. Sprinkle, 1 tablespoon at a time, 4 to 5 tablespoons of the milk over the flour mixture, lightly mixing with a fork after each addition, to form a firm dough.

Preheat the oven to 375°F. Roll out dough and cut into 3-inch squares. Place a rounded teaspoonful of the cooled filling in the center of each pastry square. Moisten the pastry edges with water. Fold the pastry in half to form a triangle, pressing the edges to seal. Prick the tops of the turnovers and brush with the remaining milk. Sprinkle with a little sugar and arrange on an ungreased baking sheet. Bake for 12 to 15 minutes, or until browned and flaky. Remove from the baking sheet and cool completely on wire racks.

Raisin-Nut Cups

30 candies

These dainty candies are quick to make and delicious. Serve them in elegant little candy papers sold as "petit four cases" for a professional look, or roll them into balls.

1/4 cup Sun-Maid® Puffed
Seeded Muscat Raisins,
chopped
2 tablespoons dark rum
1/2 cup sugar

1/2 cup semisweet chocolate
pieces
1 cup minced or ground
walnuts
Small walnut pieces

Combine the raisins and rum. Cover, and let stand several hours or overnight. (Or warm the raisins and rum for 1 to 2 minutes; let stand a few minutes before using.)

In a small saucepan, boil the sugar and 1/4 cup water for 2 minutes. Reduce heat and stir in the chocolate pieces until melted and smooth. Stir in the minced walnuts and the raisin mixture. Spoon into tiny paper or foil petit four cases. Garnish with walnut pieces. Refrigerate until firm.

Variation

Raisin-Nut Balls: To roll the mixture into balls, increase minced walnuts to 1 1/2 cups. Cool chocolate mixture until cool enough to handle. Shape rounded teaspoonfuls of the mixture into balls. Roll in confectioners sugar. Chill.

Hermits   36 cookies

These cookies are perennial favorites and bridge the generation gap.

1/2 cup butter or margarine,
    softened
1 cup firmly packed light
    brown sugar
2 eggs
2 cups all-purpose flour
1 teaspoon baking soda

1 teaspoon nutmeg
1/2 teaspoon cinnamon
1/2 teaspoon salt
1 cup Sun-Maid® Seedless
    Raisins
1/2 cup coarsely chopped
    walnuts

Preheat the oven to 375°F. Grease a baking sheet. Cream the butter and sugar until light and fluffy. Beat in the eggs until smooth. Combine the flour, baking soda, nutmeg, cinnamon, and salt and stir into the butter mixture. Stir in the raisins and walnuts. Drop batter by rounded teaspoonfuls onto the prepared sheet, leaving about 1 1/2 inches between cookies. Bake for 12 minutes, or until lightly browned. Gently remove the cookies to a wire rack to cool.

Apricot-Pineapple Jam   8 8-ounce jars

A luscious and easily prepared jam that is perfect for gift-giving or everyday family pleasure.

1 1/4 cups dried apricots
1 can (20 ounces) crushed
    pineapple
6 cups sugar
1/2 cup lemon juice

1/2 (6 ounce) bottle liquid
    fruit pectin
1/3 cup slivered maraschino
    cherries, well drained

Combine the apricots with 2 cups water and let stand 4 hours, or overnight. Strain the liquid into a large saucepan. Finely chop the apricots. Add the apricots to the saucepan along with the pineapple, sugar, and lemon juice and bring to a full rolling boil over high heat, stirring constantly. Boil for 1 minute stirring constantly; remove from heat and stir in pectin and cherries. Skim off foam. Stir and skim for 5 minutes. Ladle into hot, sterilized jars. Seal at once.

Hiker's Special

about 4 3/4 cups

1 cup Sun-Maid® Seedless
    Raisins
3/4 cup date bits
1/2 cup dried pineapple pieces
1/2 cup dried apple pieces

1/2 cup whole almonds
1/2 cup filberts
1/2 cup dry-roasted peanuts
1/2 cup pepitas
    (pumpkin seeds)

Combine all ingredients. Toss well. Store in tightly covered container.

Natural Energy Combo

about 3 1/2 cups

1 cup almond pieces
3/4 cup Sun-Maid® Seedless
    Raisins
1/2 cup Sun-Maid® Seedless
    Golden Raisins
1/2 cup carob chips or
    semi-sweet chocolate
    pieces

1/2 cup walnut pieces
1/4 cup sunflower seeds
2 tablespoons chopped
    dried apricot

Combine all ingredients. Toss well. Store in tightly covered container.

Rugelach

24 rolls

"Miniature Danish rolls" is the perfect description of these flaky little swirls. Serve them warm with coffee.

1 cup butter or margarine,
    softened
1 package (8 ounces) cream
    cheese, at room
    temperature
2 cups all-purpose flour
1/8 teaspoon salt

2/3 cup Sun-Maid® Zante
    Currants or Sun-Maid®
    Puffed Seeded Muscat
    Raisins, chopped
1/2 cup chopped walnuts
1/2 teaspoon cinnamon
2 tablespoons sugar

Combine the butter and cream cheese. Add flour and salt and knead by hand or beat until well mixed and smooth. Divide dough in half. Wrap each half and refrigerate until dough is well chilled, several hours or overnight. Combine currants, walnuts, cinnamon, and sugar. On lightly floured board, roll each dough half into a 12×8-inch rectangle. Sprinkle each rectangle with half of the currant mixture, to within about 1/4 inch of the edges.

Preheat oven to 350°F. Starting with the 12-inch side, roll dough into a long tube. Moisten the edge with water and pinch seam lightly to hold in place. Cut into 1-inch-thick slices and place on lightly greased baking sheet. Bake for 18 to 20 minutes, or until pastry is very lightly browned. Remove from pan and cool slightly on wire rack.

Raisin Cocktail Nibblers   8 cups

A crunchy snack to serve with drinks or to leave out for after-school treats.

1/2 cup butter or margarine	2 cups small cereal wheat
1 tablespoon Worcestershire	squares
sauce	2 cups small cereal rice
1 teaspoon chili powder	squares
1/2 teaspoon seasoned salt	1 1/2 cups Sun-Maid® Seedless
1 cup salted peanuts	Raisins
2 cups thin pretzel sticks	

Heat the butter with the Worcestershire, chili powder, and seasoned salt in a small saucepan until melted and smooth. In a large bowl, combine the peanuts, pretzels, and cereal squares. Preheat the oven to 250°F. Pour the seasoned butter over the cereal mixture in a thin stream, tossing lightly with a fork as you pour. Stir until all the pieces are coated. Spread the nibblers in a large shallow pan and bake for 45 minutes, stirring occasionally. Add the raisins and bake 15 minutes longer. Cool completely. Store in a tightly covered container.

Raisin Tartlets   24 tartlets

It's hard to believe that you can cram so many good things into such tiny packages.

Cream Cheese Pastry	1/2 teaspoon vanilla extract
(below)	Dash salt
1 egg, beaten	1/3 cup Sun-Maid® Puffed
3/4 cup firmly packed light	Seeded Muscat Raisins,
brown sugar	chopped
1 tablespoon butter,	1/3 cup semisweet chocolate
softened	pieces
1/2 teaspoon grated orange peel	1/3 cup chopped pecans

Divide the pastry into 24 pieces. Chill dough. Press into 1 3/4-inch muffin cups. Preheat the oven to 350°F. Beat the egg with the brown sugar, butter, orange peel, vanilla, and salt until smooth. Stir in the raisins, chocolate pieces, and pecans. Spoon the filling into the pastry-lined muffin cups. Bake for 25 minutes. Let stand 10 minutes on a wire rack before removing the tartlets from the cups to cool completely.

Cream Cheese Pastry   1 9-inch pie shell
                                                  or 24 tartlet shells

1 package (3 ounces) cream	1/2 cup margarine,
cheese, at room	softened
temperature	1 cup all-purpose flour

Cut the cream cheese and butter into the flour with a pastry blender or the fingertips. Work until the mixture forms a smooth dough.

Cracked-Wheat Cookies   36 cookies

Here's a raisin-studded cookie that won't be around the house for long.

1/2 cup bulgur	1 1/4 cups all-purpose flour
1/2 cup butter or margarine,	3/4 teaspoon salt
softened	1/2 teaspoon baking soda
1/2 cup firmly packed light	1/2 teaspoon vanilla extract
or dark brown sugar	1 cup Sun-Maid® Seedless
1 egg	Raisins

Pour hot water to cover over the bulgur and let stand for 15 to 20 minutes. Drain well. Grease 2 baking sheets. Preheat the oven to 375°F. In a large mixer bowl, cream the butter and brown sugar until fluffy. Beat in the egg. Combine the flour, salt, and baking soda. Reduce speed to low and beat the dry ingredients into the butter and sugar mixture. Stir in the vanilla and raisins. Stir the well-drained bulgur into the cookie batter. Drop by rounded teaspoons onto the prepared sheets. Bake for 12 minutes, or until golden brown. Cool on wire racks.

Lemon Apricot Sauce   1 1/2 cups

Serve this sauce over anything from pancakes for breakfast to baba au rhum for dessert.

1/4 cup (about 10) dried apricots	3 tablespoons lemon juice
1/4 cup Sun-Maid® Seedless	1 stick cinnamon
Golden Raisins	1/8 teaspoon salt
1/2 cup sugar	

In a medium-size saucepan, combine all ingredients with 1 1/2 cups water and bring to a boil. Reduce heat, cover, and simmer for 15 minutes. Let stand until lukewarm. Remove the cinnamon stick and pour the apricot mixture into a blender container or food processor. Cover and process until smooth. If necessary, add a little more water to thin the sauce to the desired consistency. Serve warm or at room temperature. (The sauce will thicken slightly when chilled.)

Raisin Jam   6 8-ounce jars

Make this wonderful jam at any time of the year.

2 cups Sun-Maid® Puffed	1 tablespoon grated
Seeded Muscat Raisins	lemon peel
1 package (1 3/4 to 2 ounces)	1 1/2 teaspoons cinnamon
powdered fruit pectin	4 1/2 cups sugar
2 tablespoons lemon juice	

Combine the raisins with 3 cups water in a saucepan and bring to a boil. Cover and simmer for 3 minutes, then let stand a few minutes to cool slightly. Pour into a blender container or food processor, cover, and process until relatively smooth. (Or force through a food mill.) Measure purée; if necessary, add water to make 4 cups.

Turn the puree into a 6-quart heavy saucepan with the pectin, lemon juice, lemon peel, and cinnamon. Bring to a boil, stirring constantly. Add the sugar. Bring to a full rolling boil, stirring constantly, and boil 1 minute. Remove from heat. Skim off foam; continue to stir and skim for about 5 minutes. Ladle into hot, sterilized jars. Seal immediately.

Sherried Apricot Sauce   1 3/4 cups

Serve this simple sauce warm over ice cream or a plain dessert; glaze a cake with it; or use it to baste meat. It's as versatile as it is delicious.

1/2 cup (about 20) dried apricots	1/4 teaspoon salt
1/2 cup firmly packed light brown sugar	2 to 3 tablespoons medium-dry sherry

Combine the apricots, sugar, and salt with 1 1/2 cups water in a medium-size saucepan, and bring to a boil. Reduce heat and simmer, uncovered, for 15 to 20 minutes, or until the apricots are very tender. Stir in the sherry. Pour into a food processor (using chopping blade) or container of a blender. Cover and process until smooth.

This sauce is good hot or cold and will keep for up to 2 weeks in the refrigerator.

Apricot-Sesame Bars   16 bars

A nourishing bar cookie that's been rated "Super!" in all taste tests.

1/2 cup sesame seed	1/2 teaspoon baking soda
3/4 cup butter or margarine, softened	1/2 teaspoon cinnamon
1 cup firmly packed light brown sugar	1 cup rolled oats
1 egg	1 cup finely chopped dried apricots
1 cup all-purpose flour	1/2 cup Sun-Maid® Puffed Seeded Muscat Raisins, chopped
1/2 teaspoon salt	

Preheat the oven to 350°F. Spread the sesame seed in a shallow pan and bake, stirring occasionally, for 5 to 8 minutes, or until golden. Grease a 13×9×2-inch baking pan. In a large mixer bowl, cream the butter, brown sugar, and egg until light and fluffy. Stir in the flour, salt, baking soda, and cinnamon until well mixed. Add the oats, apricots, toasted sesame seed, and raisins. Mix well; the batter will be thick. Spread the batter evenly in the prepared baking pan and bake for 25 minutes, or until the top springs back when lightly pressed. Cool before cutting into bars.

Apricot-Raisin Conserve

4 8-ounce jars

A quick-cooking conserve that tastes as if it had been prepared in an old-fashioned kitchen.

2 1/2 cups (about 12 ounces)
  dried apricots
2 cups sugar
1 1/2 cups Sun-Maid® Golden
  Raisins
1/3 cup lemon juice

2 teaspoons grated
  lemon peel
1 1/2 cups chopped toasted
  almonds
1/2 teaspoon almond extract

Cover the apricots with 3 cups water and let stand for 4 hours or overnight. Strain the liquid into a saucepan, and finely chop the apricots, adding them to the pan with the sugar, raisins, lemon juice, and lemon peel. Cook over medium heat, stirring constantly, until the mixture comes to a boil. Simmer, stirring occasionally, about 30 minutes, or until the conserve is thick and clear. Stir in the almonds and almond extract. Boil 1 minute longer. Remove from heat and ladle into hot, sterilized jars. Seal immediately.

Rum Raisin Sauce

1 3/4 cups

Spoon this fragrant sauce over ice cream, rice pudding, or slices of pound or spice cake.

1 large orange,
  juice and grated peel
1 tablespoon cornstarch
1/2 cup honey or corn syrup
1/4 cup firmly packed brown
  sugar

1/8 teaspoon salt
1/2 cup Sun-Maid® Seedless
  Raisins, chopped
2 to 3 tablespoons
  dark rum

Combine the orange juice and peel with 2/3 cup water in a saucepan; stir in the cornstarch. Add the honey, brown sugar, and salt. Bring to a boil, stirring constantly. Reduce heat and simmer, uncovered, 5 minutes. Add the raisins and cook 1 minute longer. Remove from heat and stir in the rum to taste. Serve warm or at room temperature.

Ginger Apricot Sauce

3/4 cup

Just the sauce to serve with oriental food or to add spice and flavor to meat dishes.

1/4 cup (about 10)
  dried apricots
1/4 cup sugar

1 teaspoon ginger
1/4 teaspoon salt
1 tablespoon lemon juice

Combine the apricots, sugar, ginger, and salt with 3/4 cup water in a small saucepan and bring to a boil. Reduce heat and simmer, uncovered, for 5 minutes. Pour the mixture into a blender container or food processor. Add the lemon juice, cover, and process until smooth. Serve warm.

Index

A TASTEFUL GIFT IDEA: GIVE A FRIEND A SUN·MAID® COOKBOOK AND SAVE.

Now that you've had a chance to enjoy the recipes in this cookbook, don't keep them a secret. The Sun-Maid Cookbook is a perfect gift idea, so give one to a friend. The spiral-bound book is only $2.00 ($4.95 value) and the hardcover one is only $4.00 ($6.95 value). So send in the attached order blank now. It'll make a friend happy.

SAVE 10¢ ON SUN·MAID® RAISINS.

Now that you know all the delicious recipes you can create with Sun-Maid Raisins, get a package and get started. You'll save 10¢ on any package of Sun-Maid Raisins with the coupon above.

©Sun-Maid Growers of California, 1980